THE YEA
WERE]

1942

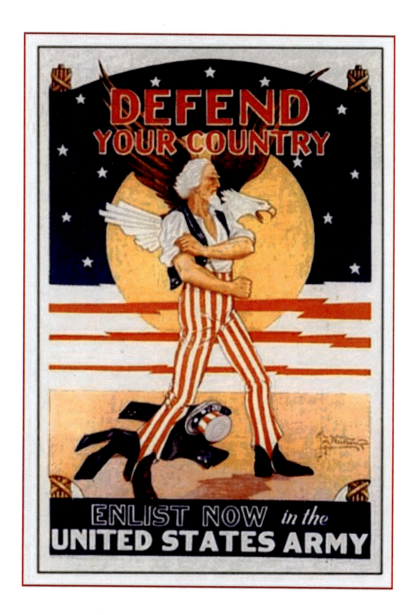

A fascinating book about the year 1942 with information on History of America, Events of the year USA, Adverts of 1942, Cost of living, Births, Sporting events, Book publications, Movies, Music, World events and People in power.

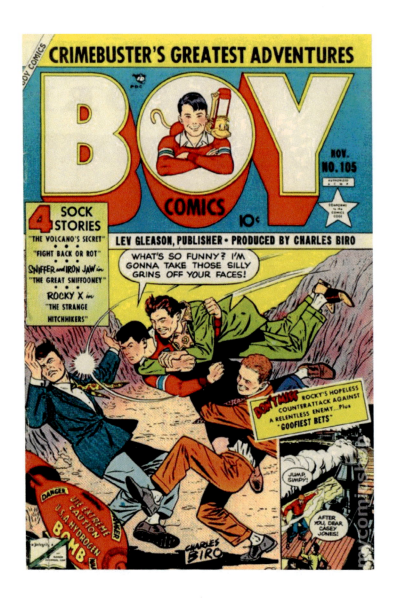

INDEX

HISTORY OF AMERICA IN 1942

Joining the military

The United States faced a mammoth job in December 1941. Ill-equipped and wounded, the nation was at war with three formidable adversaries. It had to prepare to fight on two distant and very different fronts, Europe and the Pacific.

America needed to quickly raise, train, and outfit a vast military force. At the same time, it had to find a way to provide material aid to its hard-pressed allies in Great Britain and the Soviet Union.

Meeting these challenges would require massive government spending, conversion of existing industries to wartime production, construction of huge new factories, changes in consumption, and restrictions on many aspects of American life. Government, industry, and labor would need to cooperate. Contributions from all Americans, young and old, men and women, would be necessary to build up what President Roosevelt called the "Arsenal of Democracy."

In the months after Pearl Harbor, the nation swiftly mobilized its human and material resources for war. The opportunities and sacrifices of wartime would change America in profound, and sometimes unexpected, ways.

Recruitment

The primary task facing America in 1941 was raising and training a credible military force. Concern over the threat of war had spurred President Roosevelt and Congress to approve the nation's first peacetime military draft in September 1940. By December 1941 America's military had grown to nearly 2.2 million soldiers, sailors, airmen, and marines.

America's armed forces consisted largely of "citizen soldiers", men and women drawn from civilian life. They came from every state in the nation and all economic and social strata.

Many were volunteers, but the majority, roughly 10 million, entered the military through the draft. Most draftees were assigned to the army. The other services attracted enough volunteers at first, but eventually their ranks also included draftees.

Barracks Life

Upon their arrival at the training camps, inductees were stripped of the freedom and individuality they had enjoyed as civilians. They had to adapt to an entirely new way of living, one that involved routine inspections and strict military conduct, as well as rigorous physical and combat training. They were given identical haircuts, uniforms, and equipment, and were assigned to Spartan barracks that afforded no privacy and little room for personal possessions.

The Draft

By late 1942 all men aged 18 to 64 were required to register for the draft, though in practice the system concentrated on men under 38. Eventually 36 million men registered. Individuals were selected from this manpower pool for examination by one of over 6,000 local draft boards. These boards, comprised of citizens from individual communities, determined if a man was fit to enter the military. They considered factors like the importance of a man's occupation to the war effort, his health, and his family situation. Many men volunteered rather than wait to be drafted. That way, they could choose their branch of service.

Potential servicemen reported to military induction centers to undergo physical and psychiatric examinations. If a man passed these exams, he was fingerprinted and asked which type of service he preferred, though his assignment would be based on the military's needs. After signing his induction papers, he was issued a serial number. The final step was the administration of the oath. He was now in the military. After a short furlough, he reported to a reception center before being shipped to a training camp. New recruits faced more medical examinations, inoculations, and aptitude tests.

Training

The training camp was the forge in which civilians began to become military men and women. In the training camps new servicemen and women underwent rigorous physical conditioning. They were drilled in the basic elements of military life and trained to work as part of a team. They learned to operate and maintain weapons. They took tests to determine their talents and were taught more specialized skills. Paratroopers, antiaircraft teams, desert troops, and other unique units received additional instruction at special training centers.

The Home Front

Raising an armed force was just part of America's war effort. That force had to be supplied with the uniforms, guns, tanks, ships, warplanes, and other weapons and equipment needed to fight. With its vast human and material resources, the United States had the potential to supply both itself and its allies. But first the American economy had to be converted to war production.

The war production effort brought immense changes to American life. As millions of men and women entered the service and production boomed, unemployment virtually disappeared. The need for labor opened up new opportunities for women and African Americans and other minorities. Millions of Americans left home to take jobs in war plants that sprang up around the nation. Economic output skyrocketed.

The war effort on the "Home Front" required sacrifices and cooperation. "Don't you know there's a war on?" was a common expression. Rationing became part of everyday life. Americans learned to conserve vital resources. They lived with price controls, dealt with shortages of everything from nylons to housing, and volunteered for jobs ranging from air raid warden to Red Cross worker.

Rationing and Recycling

"Food for Victory"

To conserve and produce more food, a "Food for Victory" campaign was launched. Eating leftovers became a patriotic duty and civilians were urged to grow their own vegetables and fruits. Millions of "Victory gardens," planted and maintained by ordinary citizens, appeared in backyards, vacant lots, and public parks. They produced over 1 billion tons of food. Americans canned food at home and consulted "Victory cookbooks" for recipes and tips to make the most of rationed goods.

"Make It Do or Do Without"

War production created shortages of critical supplies. To overcome these shortages, war planners searched for substitutes. One key metal in limited supply was copper. It was used in many war-related products, including assault wire. The military needed millions of miles of this wire to communicate on battlefields.

To satisfy the military's demands, copper substitutes had to be found to use in products less important to the nation's defense. The US Mint helped solve the copper shortage. During 1943 it made pennies out of steel. The Mint also conserved nickel, another important metal, by removing it from 5-cent coins. Substitutions like these helped win the production battle.

"Do with Less, So They'll Have More"

The military needed more than guns and ammunition to do its job. It had to be fed. The Army's standard K ration included chocolate bars, which were produced in huge numbers. Cocoa production was increased to make this possible. Sugar was another ingredient in chocolate. It was also used in chewing gum, another part of the K ration. Sugar cane was needed to produce gunpowder, dynamite, and other chemical products. To satisfy the military's needs, sugar was rationed to civilians. The government also rationed other foods, including meat and coffee. Local rationing boards issued coupons to consumers that entitled them to a limited supply of rationed items.

"Save Waste Fat for Explosives"

Ammunition for rifles, artillery, mortars, and other weapons was one of the most important manufacturing priorities of World War II. A key ingredient needed to make the explosives in much ammunition was glycerin.

To help produce more ammunition, Americans were encouraged to save household waste fat, which was used to make glycerin. Other household goods, including rags, paper, silk, and string, were also recycled. This was a home front project that all Americans could join.

Salvage for Victory

Canteens are a standard part of military equipment. Millions were produced during the war. Most were made of steel or aluminum, metals which were also used to make everything from ammunition to ships. At times, both metals were in short supply. To meet America's metal needs, scrap was salvaged from basements, backyards, and attics. Old cars, bed frames, radiators, pots, and pipes were just some of the items gathered at metal "scrap drives" around the nation. Americans also collected rubber, tin, nylon, and paper at salvage drives.

"Share Your Cars and Spare Your Tires"

America's military needed millions of tires for jeeps, trucks, and other vehicles. Tires required rubber. Rubber was also used to produce tanks and planes. But when Japan invaded Southeast Asia, the United States was cut off from one of its chief sources of this critical raw product. America overcame its rubber shortage in several ways. Speed limits and gas rationing forced people to limit their driving. This reduced wear and tear on tires. A synthetic rubber industry was created. The public also carpooled and contributed rubber scrap for recycling.

MOBILIZING THE ECONOMY

America's economy performed astonishing feats during World War II. Manufacturers retooled their plants to produce war goods. But this alone was not enough. Soon huge new factories, built with government and private funds, appeared around the nation. Millions of new jobs were created and millions of Americans moved to new communities to fill them. Annual economic production, as measured by the Gross National Product (GNP), more than doubled, rising from $99.7 billion in 1940 to nearly $212 billion in 1945.

Production Miracles In industry after industry Americans performed production miracles. One story helps capture the scale of the defense effort. In 1940 President Roosevelt shocked Congress when he proposed building 50,000 aircraft a year. In 1944 the nation made almost double that number. Ford's massive Willow Run bomber factory alone produced nearly one plane an hour by March 1944.

To achieve increases like this, defense spending jumped from $1.5 billion in 1940 to $81.5 billion in 1945. By 1944 America led the world in arms production, making more than enough to fill its military needs. At the same time, the United States was providing its allies in Great Britain and the Soviet Union with critically needed supplies.

HIGGINS BOATS
Higgins Industries designed and built two basic classes of military craft.

The first was landing craft, constructed of wood and steel and used to transport fully armed troops, light tanks, field artillery, and other mechanized equipment and supplies to shore. These boats helped make the amphibious landings of World War II possible.

Higgins also designed and manufactured supply vessels and specialized patrol craft, including high-speed PT boats, antisubmarine boats, and dispatch boats.

U.S. EVENTS OF 1942

January

1 The Oregon State Beavers defeated the Duke Blue Devils 20–16 in the 28th Rose Bowl game. The venue was moved from Rose Bowl Stadium in Pasadena, California, to the Blue Devils' home stadium in Durham, North Carolina, due to fears about a Japanese attack on the U.S. West Coast.

2 The marriage of Dorothy Thompson and Sinclair Lewis was legally dissolved. She was the first American journalist to be expelled from Nazi Germany in 1934 and was one of the few women news commentators on radio during the 1930s. Thompson is regarded by some as the "First Lady of American Journalism" and was recognized by Time magazine in 1939 as equal in influence to Eleanor Roosevelt.

4 The fourth National Football League All-Star Game was held at the Polo Grounds in New York City. The Chicago Bears defeated an all-star team 35–24. The game was originally scheduled to be held in Los Angeles where the first three all-star games were held, but it was moved to New York due to wartime travel restrictions.

6 U.S. President Franklin D. Roosevelt gave the State of the Union Address to Congress. "In fulfilling my duty to report upon the State of the Union, I am proud to say to you that the spirit of the American people was never higher than it is today—the Union was never more closely knit together—this country was never more deeply determined to face the solemn tasks before it", the president began. "The response of the American people has been instantaneous, and it will be sustained until our security is assured ... We have not been stunned. We have not been terrified or confused. This very reassembling of the Seventy-seventh Congress today is proof of that; for the mood of quiet, grim resolution which here prevails bodes ill for those who conspired and collaborated to murder world peace. That mood is stronger than any mere desire for revenge. It expresses the will of the American people to make very certain that the world will never so suffer again."

7 U.S. President Franklin D. Roosevelt presented Congress with the biggest budget ever seen up to that time. It called the expenditure of $77 billion over the next 18 months, $56 billion of which was for the war effort. The plan called for the production of 125,000 aircraft, 75,000 tanks, 35,000 guns and 8 million tons of shipping by the end of 1943.

9 Joe Louis knocked out Buddy Baer in the first round at Madison Square Garden to retain the World Heavyweight Boxing Championship.

10 Movie stars Mickey Rooney and Ava Gardner were married at a Protestant church in Ballard, California.

11 The American cargo ship USAT Liberty was torpedoed by Japanese submarine I-166 and beached on the island of Bali.

12 Joe Louis reported for duty at Camp Upton. A large contingent of reporters turned up to make photographs and newsreel film of the boxing champion in uniform.

15 President Roosevelt sent a letter to baseball commissioner Kenesaw Mountain Landis saying that baseball should continue in wartime. "I honestly feel that it would be best for the country to keep baseball going", Roosevelt wrote. "There will be fewer people unemployed and everybody will work longer hours and harder than ever before. And that means that they ought to have a chance for recreation and for taking their minds off their work even more than before."

16 TWA Flight 3 crashed into a cliff on Potosi Mountain in Nevada shortly after takeoff during a passenger flight to Burbank, California. All 19 passengers and 3 crew aboard were killed, including the actress Carole Lombard and her mother.

19 United States VIII Bomber Command was established. It is headquartered at Barksdale Air Force Base, Louisiana. The command serves as Air Forces Strategic – Global Strike, one of the air components of United States Strategic Command (USSTRATCOM). The Eighth Air Force includes the heart of America's heavy bomber force: The B-2 Spirit stealth bomber, the B-1 Lancer supersonic bomber, and the B-52 Stratofortress heavy bomber aircraft.

20 The American submarine S-36 ran aground on the Taka Bakang Reef in the Makassar Strait and was scuttled the following day.

23 The war film Joan of Paris starring Michèle Morgan and Paul Henreid premiered in New York City.

24 A committee assigned by President Roosevelt on December 18, 1941 to investigate the Pearl Harbor attack issued its report, putting the blame on Admiral Husband E. Kimmel and Lieutenant General Walter Short for failing to coordinate their defenses appropriately or taking measures reasonably required in the light of the warnings they had been given. Both men would receive death threats as a result of the report.

26 The first American soldiers to land in the European theatre of operations disembarked at Belfast, Northern Ireland. Their arrival was kept a secret right up until the first ship docked.

28 The ninth Pan-American Conference adjourned after the representatives of 21 countries signed an agreement to sever diplomatic, financial and commercial relations with the Axis powers.

29 The U.S. Coast Guard ship Alexander Hamilton was torpedoed and sunk near Reykjavik, Iceland by the German submarine U-132.

30 The U.S. Coast and Geodetic Survey ship Pathfinder was beached at Corregidor after taking indirect damage from Japanese bombing. The National Geodetic Survey's history and heritage are intertwined with those of other NOAA offices. As the U.S. Coast Survey and U.S. Coast and Geodetic Survey, the agency operated a fleet of survey ships, and from 1917 the Coast and Geodetic Survey was one of the uniformed services of the United States with its own corps of commissioned officers.

February

1 National Freedom Day was observed for the first time in the United States, commemorating Abraham Lincoln's signing of the Thirteenth Amendment to the U.S. Constitution on February 1, 1865.

2 U.S. President Franklin D. Roosevelt asked Congress to approve a $500 million loan to China.

4 United States tanker India Arrow was torpedoed and sunk about 50 nautical miles (93 km) southeast of Atlantic City by German submarine U-103.

5 United States tanker China Arrow was torpedoed, shelled and sunk about 90 nautical miles (170 km) off Delaware coast by German submarine U-103.

7 "A String of Pearls" by Glenn Miller and His Orchestra hit #1 on the Billboard singles charts.

10 The last civilian car rolled off the assembly line at the River Rouge Ford plant before the company switched production over to military vehicles such as service trucks and jeeps. Reporters and photographers were on hand to document the event.

11 The American submarine USS Shark was sunk in the Pacific Ocean by the Japanese destroyer Yamakaze.

14 American converted troopship SS President Taylor grounded on the coral reef at Canton Island and could not be salvaged despite extensive efforts.

15 President Roosevelt made a special broadcast to the people of Canada. "Yours are the achievements of a great nation," the president said after reviewing Canada's part in the war effort. "They require no praise from me-but they get that praise from me nevertheless. I understate the case when I say that we, in this country, contemplating what you have done, and the spirit in which you have done it, are proud to be your neighbors."

18 American destroyer USS Truxton and general stores issue ship Pollux ran aground at Lawn Point, Newfoundland during a storm, resulting in 110 and 93 deaths, respectively.

19 President Roosevelt signed Executive Order 9066, authorizing the internment of Japanese Americans. The internment of Japanese Americans in the United States during World War II was the forced relocation and incarceration in concentration camps in the western interior of the country of about 120,000 people of Japanese ancestry, most of whom lived on the Pacific Coast. Sixty-two percent of the internees were United States citizens. These actions were ordered by President Franklin D. Roosevelt shortly after Imperial Japan's attack on Pearl Harbor.

20 Edward O'Hare became the U.S. Navy's first flying ace.

23 President Roosevelt gave a fireside chat on the progress of the war. "We have most certainly suffered losses – from Hitler's U-Boats in the Atlantic as well as from the Japanese in the Pacific – and we shall suffer more of them before the turn of the tide," Roosevelt said. "But, speaking for the United States of America, let me say once and for all to the people of the world: We Americans have been compelled to yield ground, but we will regain it. We and the other United Nations are committed to the destruction of the militarism of Japan and Germany. We are daily increasing our strength. Soon, we and not our enemies, will have the offensive; we, not they, will win the final battles; and we, not they, will make the final peace."

February

24 | Voice of America began short-wave radio broadcasts. Its initial programmer was in German.

25 | A mysterious event called the Battle of Los Angeles took place in the early morning hours over Los Angeles, California when an anti-aircraft artillery barrage was fired into the nighttime sky. Secretary of the Navy Frank Knox called the incident a "false alarm" but offered no other information.

26 | The 14th Academy Awards were held in Los Angeles. How Green Was My Valley won Best Picture, and its director John Ford won his third Oscar for Best Director. The category Best Documentary (Short Subject) was awarded for the first time, won by the National Film Board of Canada's entry Churchill's Island.

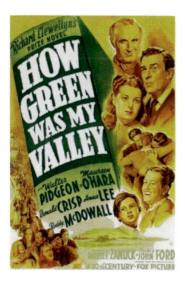  

27 | The American seaplane tender USS Langley was badly damaged south of Java by Japanese dive bombers and had to be scuttled.

28 | The United States Army Services of Supply or "SOS" branch of the U.S. Army was created.

March

1 | Near Christmas Island, the fuel tanker USS Pecos was bombed and sunk by Aichi D3A dive bombers, while the American destroyer USS Edsall was bombed and damaged by Japanese aircraft and then shelled and sunk by the battleships Hiei and Kirishima.

3 | An exhibition titled "Artists in Exile" opened at the Pierre Matisse Gallery in New York. Fourteen artists including Marc Chagall, Max Ernst, Fernand Léger and Piet Mondrian were represented at the exhibition with one piece each.

8 | The British and U.S. governments extended loans of £50 million and $500 million, respectively, to the Nationalist Chinese government.

9 | Vannevar Bush delivered a report to President Roosevelt expressing optimism on the possibility of producing an atomic bomb.

11 | Douglas MacArthur's escape from the Philippines began.

March

12

Brothers Anthony and William Esposito were executed by electric chair five minutes apart at Sing Sing Correctional Facility for the January 14, 1941 slaying of a police officer and a holdup victim, which had led to a sensational trial in which they feigned insanity. Both brothers were in such fragile health that they had to be brought into the death chamber in wheelchairs because they had refused all food for the past 10 months that was not fed them forcibly.

15

While sailing from Norfolk, Virginia to Beaumont, Texas, the United States Navy tanker Olean was torpedoed and heavily damaged by the German submarine U-158. The ship was abandoned, towed to the Hampton Roads and repaired.

16

A tornado outbreak struck a large area of the Central and Southern United States. 153 people were killed over the next two days.

17

Douglas MacArthur arrived in Australia and was appointed commander of the combined Allied forces in the southwest Pacific.

18

President Roosevelt signed Executive Order 9102, ordering the creation of the War Relocation Authority. The War Relocation Authority (WRA) was a United States government agency established to handle the internment of Japanese Americans during World War II. It also operated the Fort Ontario Emergency Refugee Shelter in Oswego, New York, which was the only refugee camp set up in the United States for refugees from Europe.

20

When reporters met the train of General Douglas MacArthur north of Adelaide, Australia, he declared: "The President of the United States ordered me to break through the Japanese lines and proceed from Corregidor to Australia for the purpose, as I understand it, of organizing the American offensive against Japan, a primary object of which is the relief of the Philippines. I came through and I shall return."

21

The spy film Secret Agent of Japan starring Preston Foster premiered at the Globe Theatre in New York City. It was the first film to include the attack on Pearl Harbor as part of the plot.

27

Joe Louis knocked out Abe Simon in the sixth round at Madison Square Garden to retain the World Heavyweight Boxing Championship.

30

The U.S. Joint Chiefs of Staff divided the Pacific theater into three areas of command: The Pacific Ocean Areas (POA), the South West Pacific Area (SWPA) and the Southeast Pacific Area.

31 The Battle of Christmas Island was fought. Japanese soldiers were able to occupy Christmas Island without resistance, although the American submarine Seawolf damaged the Japanese cruiser Naka.

April

1 The American tanker SS Tiger was torpedoed off Cape Henry, Virginia by German submarine U-754. An attempt was made to tow the Tiger but she foundered and sank in Chesapeake Bay the following day.

2 American coastal steamer David H. Atwater was controversially sunk off the U.S. east coast by gunfire from German submarine U-552.

April

3 | The action-adventure film Jungle Book starring Sabu Dastagir was released.

4 | United States tanker Byron D. Benson was torpedoed off the Carrituck Inlet by German submarine U-552. The damaged tanker finally sank on April 8.

8 | The Canadian government created the Park Steamship Company to build Park ships, the Canadian equivalent of the American Liberty ships and British Fort ships.

10 | The minesweeper USS Finch was bombed and damaged by Japanese aircraft in Manila Bay, sinking the next day and the submarine tender USS Canopus was scuttled at Mariveles, Bataan.

11 | The American steam tanker SS Gulfamerica was torpedoed and damaged off Jacksonville, Florida by the German submarine U-123, sinking five days later.

13 | The Federal Communications Commission reduced the minimum required programming time of U.S. television stations from 15 hours a week down to 4 for the duration of the war.

14 | The Father Charles Coughlin-founded periodical Social Justice was banned from the U.S. mails on charges of violating the Espionage Act of 1917 by attacking the American war effort.

18 | The Doolittle Raid was conducted by U.S. warplanes on the Japanese capital of Tokyo. Although little damage was done it provided an important boost to American morale.

19 | Warren Spahn made his major league baseball debut for the Boston Braves, retiring both of the New York Giants batters he faced.

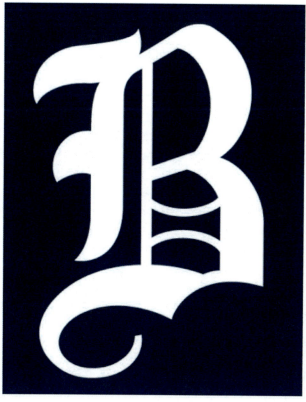

April

21 Irish-American aviator Edward O'Hare became the first naval recipient of the Medal of Honor.

22 The Allies activated Task Force 44, a naval task force in the Pacific. The task force was created on 22 April 1942 from the ANZAC Squadron as part of United States Army General Douglas MacArthur's South West Pacific Area (command). The unit's first commander was Rear Admiral John Gregory Crace (Royal Australian Navy). From 13 June 1942 the task force was commanded by Victor Crutchley, an Australian Rear Admiral of the Royal Navy (UK). The force saw action during the Battle of the Coral Sea, in which it helped turn back a Japanese attempt to invade Port Moresby, New Guinea.

24 The comedy gangster film Larceny, Inc. starring Edward G. Robinson premiered in New York City.

Edward G. Robinson   Jane Wyman

25 American troops arrived in New Caledonia to assist in defense of the archipelago.

28 A fifteen-mile strip of the Atlantic coast around New York began conducting nightly blackouts to counter German U-boat activity in the region.

29 The "Hollywood Victory Caravan", consisting of many of Hollywood's best-known entertainers, visited Washington for a gala reception on the White House lawn the day before their first show of a 30-city tour promoting the sale of war bonds. Among the many celebrities taking part were Bing Crosby, Bob Hope, Cary Grant, Desi Arnaz, Groucho Marx, Laurel and Hardy, Charles Boyer, Charlotte Greenwood, Claudette Colbert, Olivia de Havilland, Spencer Tracy and Betty Grable.

May

2 The American patrol yacht USS Cythera was torpedoed and sunk off the coast of North Carolina by the German submarine U-402.

4 The submarine rescue ship USS Pigeon and the minesweeper Tanager were sunk at Corregidor by a Japanese dive bomber and shore guns, respectively.

May

6 The American cargo ship Alcoa Puritan was torpedoed and sunk in the Gulf of Mexico off the mouth of the Mississippi River by German submarine U-507. The American gunboats Luzon, Oahu and Quail were scuttled in Manila Bay to prevent capture.

7 In the Battle of the Coral Sea, Japanese aircraft carrier Shōhō and the American destroyer Sims were sunk, while the American oiler Neosho was crippled by bombing and had to be scuttled four days later.

8 The drama film In This Our Life starring Bette Davis, Olivia de Havilland, Charles Coburn and George Brent was released.

13 The American cargo ship SS Norlantic was torpedoed and sunk in the Atlantic Ocean by the German submarine U-156.

14 U.S. intelligence partially decoded a Japanese message indicating that a large force was preparing to invade "AF". Cryptanalyst Joseph Rochefort suspected that AF represented Midway Island, but officials in Washington believed it stood for the Aleutians. The matter was settled by planting an easily readable message from Midway saying that their desalination plant had broken down. When a Japanese message was then transmitted reporting that "AF" was short of water, Rochefort's belief was confirmed.

15 The first seventeen U.S. states put gasoline rationing into effect after it became apparent that voluntary rationing was insufficient.

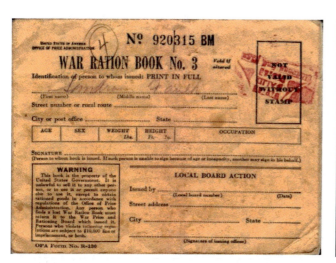

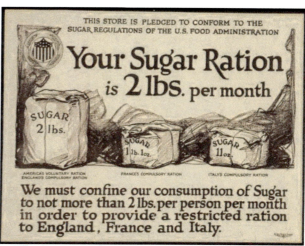

17 Japanese submarine I-28 was torpedoed and sunk off Truk by the American submarine Tautog.

20 The United States Navy signed up its first African-American recruits.

22 Townsville Mutiny: About 600 African-American servicemen mutinied in Townsville, Australia in reaction to being regularly subjected to racial abuse by some of their white officers. At least one person was killed and Australian troops were called in to roadblock the rioters.

24 A 15-minute test blackout centered on Detroit was held starting at 10 p.m., with neighboring communities such as Pontiac and Windsor, Ontario also participating. It was the largest blackout in the Midwestern United States up to that time.

May

29 | The biographical musical film Yankee Doodle Dandy starring James Cagney as the songwriter and entertainer George M. Cohan premiered in New York City. Instead of tickets, Warner Bros. sold war bonds to the premiere ranging from $25 to $25,000 in price.

30 | Fred Korematsu was arrested on a street corner in San Leandro, California after being identified as being of Japanese ancestry, despite plastic surgery on his eyelids in an attempt to pass for Caucasian. The legality of his internment would be taken all the way to the Supreme Court in the landmark case Korematsu v. United States.

June

4 | Battle of Midway – The United States Navy defeats an Imperial Japanese Navy attack against Midway Atoll.

5 | The United States declared war on the Axis satellite states of Bulgaria, Hungary and Romania.

6 | During the Battle of Midway, Japanese cruiser Mikuma was bombed and sunk by Douglas SBD Dauntless aircraft. American destroyer Hammann was torpedoed and sunk by Japanese submarine I-168.

7 | The Chicago Tribune published a front-page article titled "Navy Had Word of Jap Plan to Strike at Sea", providing clues from which the Japanese might have figured out that the Americans had broken their codes ahead of the Battle of Midway. Navy Secretary Frank Knox demanded that the Tribune be prosecuted, but once the Navy realized that the Japanese did not change their codes after the article appeared, the case was quietly dropped to avoid bringing the enemy's attention to the story.

8 | Douglas MacArthur suggested to Army Chief of Staff George Marshall that an offensive be taken in the Pacific with New Britain, New Ireland and New Guinea as the objective.

12 | Operation Pastorius: German submarine U-202 landed four saboteurs on American soil at Amagansett, New York, the first of many intended operations to sabotage economic targets within the United States.

13 | U.S. President Franklin D. Roosevelt issued Executive Order 9182, creating the Office of Strategic Services and Office of War Information.

14 | The General Electric Company in Bridgeport, Connecticut finished production on the new M1 rocket launcher, commonly known as the bazooka.

June

16 The war film Eagle Squadron starring Robert Stack, Diana Barrymore, John Loder and Nigel Bruce was released.

17 President Roosevelt signed a bill raising the minimum pay of American servicemen to $50 a month.

18 South of Jacksonville, Florida, the German submarine U-584 landed four more saboteurs as part of Operation Pastorius.

20 The comic book villain Two-Face made his first appearance in Detective Comics issue #66

21 Bombardment of Fort Stevens: An Imperial Japanese submarine fired on Fort Stevens in Oregon on the west coast of the United States.

26 President Roosevelt signed a new law prohibiting the making of unauthorized photographs or sketches of military property such as bases or ships.

27 The FBI announced the arrest of eight conspirators who planned to carry out Operation Pastorius.

July

1 The first B-17 Flying Fortress arrived in Britain. The Boeing B-17 Flying Fortress is a four-engine heavy bomber developed in the 1930s for the United States Army Air Corps. As of October 2019, 9 aircraft remain airworthy, though none of them were ever flown in combat. Dozens more are in storage or on static display.

3 The U.S. Army relaxed its draft standards to allow induction of selectees with physical deformities for limited military service.

4 The 15th Bombardment Squadron became the first USAAF unit to bomb occupied Europe when it joined the RAF in a raid on the Netherlands.

6 The American League defeated the National League 3-1 in the 10th Major League Baseball All-Star Game at the Polo Grounds in New York City. It was the first night game in All-Star history.

 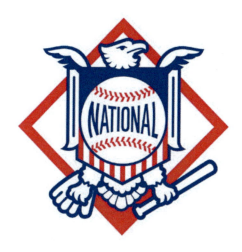

July

8 | One week after gaining U.S. citizenship, the British-born movie star Cary Grant married the socialite heiress Barbara Hutton at Lake Arrowhead, California.

10 | The Orson Welles-directed period drama film The Magnificent Ambersons starring Joseph Cotten, Dolores Costello and Anne Baxter was released.

14 | The Vichy government refused a U.S. offer to move nine warships of the French fleet to an American, neutral or Martinique port to prevent their seizure by the Axis.

15 | An American salvage crew recovered the so-called Akutan Zero intact at Akutan Island. Information gained from studying the plane allowed the Americans to devise ways to defeat the Zero.

19 | WWII – Battle of the Atlantic: German Grand Admiral Karl Dönitz orders the last U-boats to withdraw from their United States Atlantic coast positions, in response to an effective American convoy system.

27 | Lordsburg Killings: Two elderly men were shot at a Japanese-American internment camp outside of Lordsburg, New Mexico. The shooter would be charged with murder but later acquitted.

30 | WWII: A bill creating the United States Marine Corps Women's Reserve is signed into law. It was authorized by the U.S. Congress and signed into law by President Franklin D. Roosevelt on 30 July 1942. Its purpose was to release officers and men for combat, and to replace them with women in U.S. shore stations for the duration of the war, plus six months. Ruth Cheney Streeter was appointed the first director. The Reserve did not have an official nickname, as did the other World War II women's military services.

August

2 | A man named José Gallardo Díaz was found unconscious and dying on a road near a swimming hole in Commerce, California. He was rushed to hospital but died shortly after. 17 Mexican-American youths were soon arrested in a case that came to be known as the Sleepy Lagoon murder.

3 | American destroyer USS Tucker struck a mine off Espiritu Santo late in the day and sank early on August 4.

4 | The musical film Holiday Inn starring Bing Crosby and Fred Astaire with music by Irving Berlin premiered in New York City.

6 | For aiding an escaped German prisoner of war, Detroit restaurant owner Max Stephan became the first American sentenced to execution for treason since the Whiskey Rebellion in 1794.

8 | U.S. Marines captured the unfinished Japanese airbase on Guadalcanal. The base was named Henderson Field after the Battle of Midway hero Lofton R. Henderson.

9 | The New York Times Best Seller list switched from a local survey to a national one compiled from booksellers in 22 cities. The first Fiction Best Seller under the new system was And Now Tomorrow by Rachel Field.

11 Al Milnar of the Cleveland Indians and Tommy Bridges of the Detroit Tigers had one of the most epic pitchers' duels in baseball history. With the game locked in a scoreless tie in the top of the ninth inning, Milnar lost a no-hitter with two out when Doc Cramer singled to right field. Both pitchers maintained their shutouts until the fifteenth inning when the game was finally called in a 0–0 tie.

Al Milnar

Tommy Bridges

14 Dwight D. Eisenhower was named Anglo-American commander for Operation Torch. Operation Torch was an Allied invasion of French North Africa during the Second World War. While the French colonies formally aligned with Germany via Vichy France, the loyalties of the population were mixed. Reports indicated that they might support the Allies. American General Dwight D. Eisenhower, supreme commander of the Allied forces in Mediterranean Theater of Operations, planned a three-pronged attack on Casablanca (Western), Oran (Center) and Algiers (Eastern), then a rapid move on Tunis to catch Axis forces in North Africa from the west in conjunction with Allied advance from east.

August

17 The USAAF made its first air raid on occupied Europe, bombing railroad marshaling yards at Sotteville-lès-Rouen.

20 The comedy-drama film The Talk of the Town starring Cary Grant, Jean Arthur and Ronald Colman was released.

22 The American destroyer USS Ingraham sank off the coast of Nova Scotia after colliding in heavy fog with the oil tanker Chemung.

24 The Battle of the Eastern Solomon's began. The Japanese aircraft carrier Ryūjō was sunk by aircraft from USS Saratoga.

27 British and American bombers raided Rotterdam.

29 The Red Cross announced that Japan had refused free passage of ships carrying food, medicine and other necessities for American prisoners of war.

30 The U.S. Army occupied Adak Island. Runways would be constructed there over the next two weeks allowing for air strikes against the nearby Japanese-held islands of Attu and Kiska.

31 The American aircraft carrier USS Saratoga was torpedoed by the Japanese submarine I-26 and had to undergo three months of repairs.

September

1 German submarine U-756 was depth charged and sunk in the Atlantic Ocean by the Canadian corvette Morden.

7 U.S. President Franklin D. Roosevelt gave a fireside chat on inflation and the progress of the war.

8 The U.S. government shut down gold mines to release labor for the war effort.

11 The Canadian corvette HMCS Charlottetown was torpedoed and sunk in the Gulf of Saint Lawrence by the German submarine U-517.

12 Miss Texas Jo-Carroll Dennison was crowned Miss America 1942.

14 The New York Yankees clinched the American League pennant with an 8–3 win over the Cleveland Indians.

15 Near Guadalcanal the Japanese submarine I-19 fired one of the most effective torpedo salvos of the war, mortally damaging the American aircraft carrier USS Wasp and destroyer O'Brien as well as damaging the battleship North Carolina. The destroyer Lansdowne was dispatched to rescue 447 crew of the Hornet and then scuttled the carrier.

16 Laconia incident: A controversial event occurred when a USAAF B-24 Liberator attacked the U-156 while survivors rescued from the September 12 RMS Laconia sinking stood on the foredeck.

September

18	The U.S. position on Guadalcanal improved with the arrival of the 7th Marine Regiment.
21	The Boeing B-29 Superfortress had its first test flight.
24	The B&O railroad Ambassador train ran into the back of the Cleveland Express near Dickerson, Maryland, killing twelve passengers and two crewmen in the worst B&O accident since 1907.
25	The aviation-themed action film Desperate Journey starring Errol Flynn and Ronald Reagan was released.
26	The Manhattan Project was granted approval by the War Production Board to use the highest level of emergency procurement priority.
27	The St. Louis Cardinals clinched the National League pennant by defeating the Chicago Cubs 9-2 in the first game of a doubleheader.

October

1	The first Little Golden Books, a popular series of children's books, were published in the United States.
3	U.S. President Franklin D. Roosevelt ordered a freeze on wages, rents and farm prices.
5	The St. Louis Cardinals defeated the New York Yankees 4-2 to win the World Series four games to one.
8	The war film Flying Tigers starring John Wayne, John Carroll and Anna Lee was released.
9	Mob boss Roger Touhy and six others escaped from Stateville Correctional Center in Crest Hill, Illinois. Touhy and his gang would be caught a month later and he would be sentenced to an additional 199 years in prison for the escape.
11	World heavyweight boxing champion Joe Louis told reporters, "My fighting days are over."
12	The Battle of Cape Esperance ended in American victory. The American destroyer USS Duncan sank from damage inflicted by the Furutaka, but the Japanese destroyers Murakumo and Natsugumo were bombed and sunk by U.S. aircraft from Henderson Field.
13	The Japanese battleships Kongō and Haruna bombarded U.S. Marine positions on Guadalcanal for 90 minutes, causing heavy damage.
14	In one of the most significant sinking's in Canadian waters during the war, passenger ferry SS Caribou was torpedoed and sunk in the Cabot Strait by German submarine U-69. 137 of the 252 on board perished.
15	The American destroyer USS Meridith was sunk by Japanese aircraft off Guadalcanal.
16	The animated short film The Mouse of Tomorrow, featuring the debut of Mighty Mouse (as "Super Mouse"), was released in the United States.

October

18 U.S. Vice Admiral William Halsey, Jr. replaced Robert L. Ghormley as commander of the South Pacific area.

20 The American cruiser USS Chester was hit by a torpedo from the Japanese submarine I-176 southeast of San Cristóbal, killing 11 and wounding 12. Chester was able to make it to Espiritu Santo for emergency repairs.

21 A B-17 carrying Eddie Rickenbacker to conduct an inspection tour of air force facilities in the Pacific and deliver a secret message to Douglas MacArthur went missing en route from Hawaii to Canton Island. The crew had gotten lost and once the plane eventually ran out of fuel and went down, all aboard got into three small life rafts and began a 21-day ordeal drifting in the Pacific.

22 The drama film Now, Voyager starring Bette Davis, Paul Henreid and Claude Rains premiered at the Hollywood Theatre in New York City.

23 American First Lady Eleanor Roosevelt arrived in London and met with the King and Queen of England at Buckingham Palace.

25 The Japanese cruiser Yura was heavily damaged by U.S. aircraft in the Indispensable Strait off Guadalcanal and had to be scuttled.

26 During the Battle of the Santa Cruz Islands, the American aircraft carrier USS Hornet was heavily damaged by Japanese aircraft and had to be scuttled early the next day. The American destroyer USS Porter was also sunk after being hit by a torpedo.

27 The war film The Navy Comes Through starring Pat O'Brien and George Murphy had its world premiere at Treasure Island Naval Base in San Francisco Bay.

28 Clark Gable was commissioned as a second lieutenant, earning the right to regrow his famous mustache which he had to shave off when he enlisted.

31 Two days after signing his first professional contract, 21-year old Maurice Richard played in his first National Hockey League game for the Montreal Canadiens against the Boston Bruins. He recorded an assist during his first NHL shift as the Canadiens went on to win 3-2.

November

1 | U.S. forces began the Matanikau Offensive on Guadalcanal.

2 | Stars and Stripes became a daily publication, the first in U.S. Army history. Stars and Stripes is a daily American military newspaper reporting on matters concerning the members of the United States Armed Forces and their communities, with an emphasis on those serving outside the United States. It operates from inside the Department of Defense, but is editorially separate from it, and its First Amendment protection is safeguarded by the United States Congress to whom an independent ombudsman, who serves the readers' interests, regularly reports.

8 | Operation Torch – United States and United Kingdom forces land in French North Africa.

9 | WWII: U.S serviceman Edward Leonski is hanged at Melbourne's Pentridge Prison for the "Brown-Out" murders of three women in May.

10 | The Battle of Port Lyautey ended when U.S. troops captured the city's fortress and local airfield.

12 | Eddie Rickenbacker and five others were rescued in the Pacific Ocean after being lost adrift at sea for three weeks. The men had stayed alive on a diet of a few oranges retrieved from their plane when it went down, some fish they'd managed to catch and a seagull that Rickenbacker had grabbed with his bare hands.

13 | The American light cruiser Juneau was sunk at the Naval Battle of Guadalcanal. 687 men were killed in action, including the five Sullivan brothers. The Americans also lost the cruiser Atlanta and the destroyers Barton, Cushing, Laffey, Monssen and Preston, while the Japanese lost the cruiser Kinugasa and destroyers Akatsuki and Yūdachi.

15 | The American Liberty ship SS Robert E. Peary was commissioned just 4 days, 15 hours and 29 minutes after the keel was laid down.

18 | President Roosevelt ordered registration for Selective Service of all youths who had turned 18 since July 1. This made about 500,000 more Americans eligible for service.

November

21 The completion of the Alaska Highway (also known as the Alcan Highway) is celebrated (however, the "highway" is not usable by general vehicles until 1943).

23 A bill creating the United States Coast Guard Women's Reserve (SPARS) is signed into law.

26 The romantic drama film Casablanca starring Humphrey Bogart, Ingrid Bergman and Paul Henreid premiered at the Hollywood Theatre in New York City.

28 The Army–Navy Game was played in Annapolis, Maryland, with Navy defeating Army 14-0. Only 13,000 spectators saw the game because of a wartime travel restriction that only allowed residents within 10 miles of Annapolis to attend.

29 Coffee rationing began in the United States.

December

1 Fuel rationing began in the United States.

2 Manhattan Project: A team of scientists led by Enrico Fermi achieved the first self-sustained nuclear chain reaction at Chicago Pile-1.

5 Almost exactly one year after Pearl Harbor, the U.S. Navy publicly revealed the extent of losses suffered in the attack.

To solve America's manpower shortage, President Roosevelt suspended the induction of all men over age 38 into the armed forces. That same day, he transferred responsibility for all manpower issues and the Selective Service system over to the War Manpower Commission headed by Paul V. McNutt.

13 The Washington Redskins defeated the Chicago Bears 14–6 in the NFL Championship Game played at Griffith Stadium in Washington, D.C.

18 The Japanese light cruiser Tenryū was torpedoed and sunk off Madang, New Guinea by the American submarine Albacore.

25 The adventure film Arabian Nights starring Sabu, Maria Montez and Jon Hall was released.

27 On Guadalcanal, an American attempt to take Mount Asten was repulsed by the Japanese.

30 Frank Sinatra performed his first solo concert at the Paramount Theatre in New York City. Sinatra later recalled being "scared stiff" when the audience of 5,000 bobby soxers shrieked and screamed continuously for America's new teen idol.

Radio Moving Day

Saturday, March 29 will be Radio Moving Day throughout the nation, when 90 per cent of all broadcasting stations will have a new spot on the dial. Of 883 broadcasters in the country, 795 are scheduled to change. Persons with manual dialing radios will simply tune in to new stations at their new places on the dial. Quite different, however, for those owning push-button tuning radios, for they will have to have the buttons reset. There are ten million push-button radio sets in use in the United States. Radio merchants and service shops listed on this page can do the job for you, up to the minute. They give prompt, courteous, efficient services. Their prices are reasonable.

FREE! FREE!!
NEW RADIO LOG BOOK OF ALL BROADCASTING STATIONS
Your Radio Will Always Play Right When Serviced by
Badger Radio Service
PROMPT SERVICE

THOMAS AND ARNOLD RADIO and RECORD SHOP
ALL MAKES OF RADIOS REPAIRED

FREE RADIO STATION FINDER
GOSHEN'S RADIO SERVICE

GLOBE RADIO & SOUND SERVICE

A. D. C. RADIO SHOP
W. W. Lewis, Electrical Engineer
4243 HASTINGS ST.

LET EDDIE
4761 Hastings

MUSIC STORE
LATEST RECORDS 3 FOR $1.00
2932 Hastings

COMPLETE RADIO SERVICE
REPAIR SPECIALISTS

FRIEDENBERG FURNITURE HOUSE, INC.
Furniture, Rugs, Stoves and Radios

Modern Style Note
OLD-FASHIONED RUNNING BOARDS ARE OUT!

Again CHEVROLET'S THE LEADER!

makes LIGHT work of BRIGHT ideas

Del Monte FRUIT COCKTAIL
— the brand that puts flavor first

DELRICH
E-Z COLOR PAK MARGARINE
ENDS MIXING BOWL MESS!

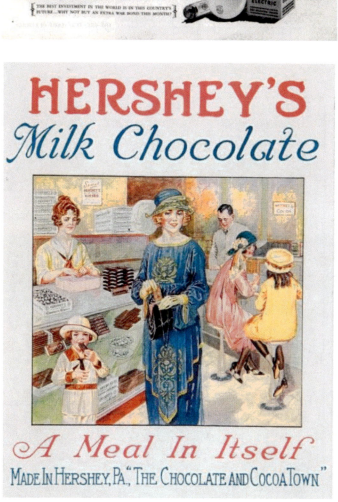

29

COST OF LIVING 1942

Wages	**$1,885.00**
House price	$3,775.00
House rental	**$35.00 per month**
New Car	$920.00
First class stamp	**3 cents**
Min wage	**30cents per hour**
Gallon of gas	**15 cents**
Apples, Pippins 2lb	25 cents
Bacon sliced 1lb	**28 cents**
Chewing Gum	26 cents for 5-pound bag
Flour	**57 cents per pound**
Bread per loaf	9 cents
Milk	**28 cents per gallon**
Eggs	34 cents per dozen
Bottle of Cola	**5 cents**
Butter	43 cents per pound
Potatoes	**32 cents per pound**
Coffee	24 cents per pound

In 1942 the price of gold was $33.85 an ounce and as of 2020 the price is $1,888.04.
Prices vary by state and the average is taken

30

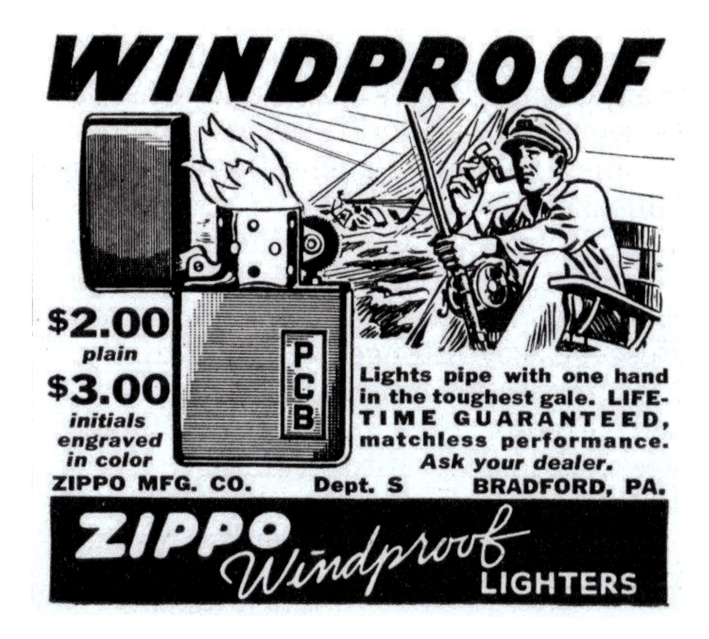
A Zippo lighter is a reusable metal lighter manufactured by American Zippo Manufacturing Company of Bradford, Pennsylvania, United States of America. Thousands of different styles and designs have been made in the eight decades since their introduction including military versions for specific regiments. Since its invention, Zippos have been sold around the world and have been described "a legendary and distinct symbol of America".

Zippo lighters became popular in the United States military, especially during World War II—when, as the company's web site says, Zippo "ceased production of lighters for consumer markets and dedicated all manufacturing to the US military". Period Zippos were made of brass, but Zippo used a black crackle finished steel during the war years because of metal shortages. While the Zippo Manufacturing Company never had an official contract with the military, soldiers and armed forces personnel insisted that base exchange (BX) and post exchange (PX) stores carry this sought-after lighter. While it had previously been common to have Zippos with authorized badges, unit crests, and division insignias, it became popular among the American soldiers of the Vietnam War to get their Zippos engraved with personal mottos. These lighters are now sought-after collector's items and popular souvenirs for visitors to Vietnam.

America's final bill for the fighting in the Pacific and Europe was massive. In today's dollars, World War II cost $4.1 trillion, according to data from the Congressional Research Service.

That's about equal to the value of either of today's two largest companies — Apple or Amazon — four times over.

How does that compare to the cost of modern wars? A Pentagon report says the U.S. has spent "only" $1.5 trillion on America's longest war, the war in Afghanistan, plus related anti-terror campaigns in Iraq and Syria.

To help finance the war, U.S. income taxes were raised to the highest levels in history.

For 1944 and 1945, income amounts above $200,000 — about $2.8 million in today's dollars — were taxed at an astounding marginal tax rate of 94%! After the war, that top rate was brought down to 91%.

Today, the top marginal income tax rate is 37%. It had been 39.6% but was cut to the current level by the December 2017 tax law.

The Japanese attack on Pearl Harbor on Dec. 7, 1941, prolonged a Wall Street funk that had begun with the notorious stock market crash of 1929.

The Dow Jones industrial average went into a downward spiral, and by late April 1942 it was at its lowest level since 1934. But then things began to turn around.

Investor's Business Daily speculates investors concluded that the U.S. would win the war. Bullishness carried the Dow up 130% over the next four years.

Heading into World War II, the military was not a career choice that paid well. Before the Pearl Harbor attack in late 1941, privates earned $21 per month. In today's money, that works out to a salary of about $4,100 a year.

But in September 1942, the pay rate for a private more than doubled, to $50 a month. Because the U.S. was still emerging from the Depression, that was better than what many civilian professional men were making.

The comparatively high military pay was necessary to draw a large percentage of the male population into the war effort.

U.S. military spending surged over the course of the war.

The annual defense budget rose from $1.9 billion in 1940 to $59.8 billion by 1945, according to Mitchell Bard in The Complete Idiot's Guide to World War II.

In 1943, the U.S. spent more than one and a half times on defense than Germany did, and more than 10 times what Japan was spending.

The U.S. military needed lots of metal, to build tanks, planes, ships, guns and even tins for soldiers' food rations. Metals shortages prompted people on the home front to collect old pots, pans, cans and various scrap metal for recycling.

As copper became scarce, the U.S. Mint made its 1943 Lincoln pennies out of steel coated with zinc. They're the only Lincoln cents that look silver, instead of the familiar reddish color.

AMERICAN BIRTHS OF 1942

Charles Peete Rose Jr. born January 5, 1942 is an American retired television journalist and talk show host. From 1991 to 2017, he was the host and executive producer of the talk show Charlie Rose on PBS and Bloomberg LP. After his wife was hired by the BBC (in New York), Rose handled some assignments for the BBC on a freelance basis. In 1972, while working at New York bank Bankers Trust, Rose landed a job as a weekend reporter for WPIX-TV. Rose's "break" came in 1974, after Bill Moyers hired Rose as managing editor for the PBS series Bill Moyers' International Report. Rose worked for CBS News from 1984 to 1990 as the anchor of CBS News Nightwatch, the network's first late-night news broadcast. On September 30, 1991, Charlie Rose premiered on PBS station Thirteen/WNET and was nationally fed on PBS beginning in January 1993. In 1994, Rose moved the show to a studio owned by Bloomberg LP, which allowed for high-definition video via satellite-remote interviews. On November 15, 2011, it was announced that Rose would return to CBS to help anchor CBS This Morning.

Muhammad Ali born Cassius Marcellus Clay Jr.; January 17, 1942 and passed away June 3, 2016. He was an American professional boxer, activist, entertainer and philanthropist. Ali was born and raised in Louisville, Kentucky. He began training as an amateur boxer at age 12. At 18, he won a gold medal in the light heavyweight division at the 1960 Summer Olympics and turned professional later that year. He won the world heavyweight championship from Sonny Liston in a major upset on February 25, 1964, at age 22. On March 6, 1964, he announced that he no longer would be known as Cassius Clay but as Muhammad Ali. Ali's actions as a conscientious objector to the Vietnam War made him an icon for the larger counterculture generation and he was a very high-profile figure of racial pride for African Americans during the civil rights movement and throughout his career. He has been ranked the greatest heavyweight boxer of all time. In 1984, he made public his diagnosis of Parkinson's syndrome.

Carol Joan Klein born February 9, 1942 is an American singer-songwriter who has been active since 1958, initially as one of the staff songwriters at the Brill Building and later as a solo artist. She is the most successful female songwriter of the latter half of the 20th century in the US, having written or co-written 118 pop hits on the Billboard Hot 100. King also wrote 61 hits that charted in the UK, making her the most successful female songwriter on the UK singles charts between 1962 and 2005. Carol has made 25 solo albums, the most successful being Tapestry, which held the record for most weeks at No. 1 by a female artist for more than 20 years. Her record sales were estimated at more than 75 million copies worldwide. She has won four Grammy Awards and was inducted into the Songwriters Hall of Fame and the Rock and Roll Hall of Fame for her songwriting. She is the recipient of the 2013 Library of Congress Gershwin Prize for Popular Song, the first woman to be so honored. She is also a 2015 Kennedy Center Honoree.

John Weatherspoon born January 27, 1942 and passed away October 29, 2019 better known as John Witherspoon, was an American actor and comedian who performed in various television shows and films.

He is best remembered for his role as Willie Jones for the Friday series; Witherspoon also starred in films such as Hollywood Shuffle (1987), Boomerang (1992), The Five Heartbeats (1991), and Vampire in Brooklyn (1995). He has also made appearances on television shows such as The Fresh Prince of Bel-Air (1994), The Wayans Bros. (1995–99), The Tracy Morgan Show (2003), Barnaby Jones (1973), The Boondocks (2005–2014), and Black Jesus (2014–2019). He wrote a film, From the Old School, in which he played an elderly working man who tries to prevent a neighborhood convenience store from being developed into a strip club. John Witherspoon had a passion for music and learned to play the trumpet and French horn. John Witherspoon died of a heart attack at his home in Sherman Oaks, California, on October 29, 2019. He was 77 years old

Michael Rubens Bloomberg born February 14, 1942 is an American businessman, politician, philanthropist, and author. He is the majority owner and co-founder of Bloomberg L.P. He was the Mayor of New York City from 2002 to 2013, and was a candidate for the 2020 Democratic nomination for president of the United States.

Michael Bloomberg grew up in Medford, Massachusetts, and graduated from Johns Hopkins University and Harvard Business School. He began his career at the securities brokerage Salomon Brothers before forming his own company in 1981. That company, Bloomberg L.P., is a financial information, software and media firm that is known for its Bloomberg Terminal. Bloomberg spent the next twenty years as its chairman and CEO. In 2020, Forbes ranked him as the sixteenth-richest person in the world, with an estimated net worth of $48 billion as of April 7, 2020 and as of July 21, 2020, Bloomberg ranked 8th in Forbes 400 with net worth $60.1 billion. Since signing The Giving Pledge, Bloomberg has given away $8.2 billion.

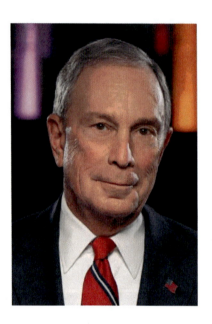

Karen Grassle born February 25, 1942 is an American actress, known for her role as Caroline Ingalls in the NBC television drama series Little House on the Prairie. She made her Broadway debut in the short-lived 1968 play The Gingham Dog. Karen Grassle auditioned for the role of the mother, Caroline Ingalls, in the Little House on the Prairie TV series and won the part. The series ran for nine seasons, from 1974 to 1983. After making the pilot for Little House on the Prairie, Grassle appeared in one episode of Gunsmoke titled "The Wiving" as Fran, one of several saloon girls kidnapped. After the series ended, she moved to Santa Fe, New Mexico and became co-founder and artistic director of Santa Fe's Resource Theater Company. Later she moved to Louisville, Kentucky, where she performed with the company of actors at Actors Theatre of Louisville. Grassle continues to perform in productions in San Francisco, Berkeley, and Palo Alto as well as tours and productions such as Driving Miss Daisy in the starring role of Miss Daisy at the Manitoba Theatre Centre in Winnipeg, Manitoba, Canada.

Aretha Louise Franklin was born March 25, 1942 and died August 16, 2018. She was an American singer, songwriter, and pianist. Referred to as the "Queen of Soul", she has twice been placed 9th in Rolling Stone's 100 Greatest Artists of All Time. Franklin began her career as a child, singing gospel at New Bethel Baptist Church in Detroit, Michigan, where her father C. L. Franklin was a minister. At the age of 18, she embarked on a secular-music career as a recording artist for Columbia Records. While her career did not immediately flourish, she found acclaim and commercial success once she signed with Atlantic Records in 1966. Her commercial hits such as "I Never Loved a Man (The Way I Love You)", "Respect", "(You Make Me Feel Like) A Natural Woman", "Chain of Fools", "Think" and "I Say a Little Prayer" propelled her past her musical peers. Franklin recorded 112 charted singles on Billboard, including 77 Hot 100 entries, 17 top-ten pop singles, 100 R&B entries, and 20 number-one R&B singles. Aretha Franklin died at her home on August 16, 2018, aged 76.

Scott Wilson was born March 29, 1942 and passed away October 6, 2018. He was an American actor. He had more than 50 film credits, including In the Heat of the Night, In Cold Blood, The Great Gatsby, Dead Man Walking, Pearl Harbor, and Junebug. In 1980, Wilson received a Golden Globe nomination for Best Supporting Actor – Motion Picture for his role in William Peter Blatty's The Ninth Configuration. He played veterinarian Hershel Greene on the AMC television series The Walking Dead (2011– 2014; 2018). He also had a recurring role on CSI: Crime Scene Investigation as casino mogul Sam Braun, as well as a lead role on the Netflix series The OA as Abel Johnson. Scott Wilson was born in the small Southern town of Thomasville, Georgia. He made his screen debut portraying characters suspected of murder in his first three films. In his debut film, Wilson played a murder suspect in In the Heat of the Night (1967). Wilson appeared in Sparta Mississippi where (In the Heat of the Night) takes place, on March 15, 2014, to celebrate the city's 175th anniversary in reference to his debut appearance in the film.

Marsha Mason born April 3, 1942 is an American actress and director. She was nominated four times for the Academy Award for Best Actress: for her performances in Cinderella Liberty (1973), The Goodbye Girl (1977), Chapter Two (1979), and Only When I Laugh (1981). The first two films also won her Golden Globe Awards. She was married for ten years (1973–1983) to the playwright and screenwriter Neil Simon, who was the writer of three of her four Oscar-nominated roles. Mason's film debut was in the 1966 film Hot Rod Hullabaloo. In 1981, Mason starred along with Kristy McNichol, James Coco, and Joan Hackett in Only When I Laugh, Simon's film adaptation of his Broadway comedy-drama The Gingerbread Lady; it was another box-office success. For her performance as Georgia Hines, Mason was highly praised and earned a fourth Best Actress Oscar nomination. Mason's recent television work includes guest roles on Seinfeld, Lipstick Jungle, and Army Wives. Mason played Patricia Heaton's mother in ABC comedy series The Middle from 2010 to its conclusion in 2018.

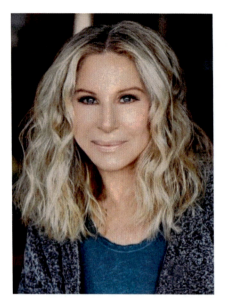

Barbara Joan "Barbra" Streisand born April 24, 1942 is an American singer, actress, and filmmaker. With a career spanning over six decades, she has achieved success in multiple fields of entertainment, and is among the few performers awarded an Emmy, Grammy, Oscar, and Tony. Following her established recording success in the 1960s, Streisand ventured into film by the end of that decade. She starred in the critically acclaimed Funny Girl (1968), for which she won the Academy Award for Best Actress. With sales exceeding 150 million records worldwide, Streisand is one of the best-selling recording artists of all time. According to the Recording Industry Association of America (RIAA), she is the highest-certified female artist in the United States, with 68.5 million certified album units tying with Mariah Carey. Her accolades include two Academy Awards, 10 Grammy Awards including the Grammy Lifetime Achievement Award and the Grammy Legend Award, five Emmy Awards, four Peabody Awards, the Presidential Medal of Freedom, and nine Golden Globes.

Tammy Wynette (born Virginia Wynette Pugh) Born May 5, 1942 and sadly passed away April 6, 1998. She was an American country music singer-songwriter and musician and was one of country music's best-known artists and biggest-selling female singers during the late 1960s and first half of the 1970s. Tammy Wynette was called the "First Lady of Country Music", and her best-known song is "Stand by Your Man." Many of her hits dealt with themes of loneliness, divorce, and the difficulties of life and relationships. During the late 1960s and early 1970s, Wynette charted 20 number-one songs on the Billboard Country Chart. Along with Loretta Lynn, Lynn Anderson, and Dolly Parton, she is credited with having defined the role of women in country music during the 1970s. Her marriage to country music singer George Jones in 1969 created a country music "couple", following the earlier success of Johnny Cash and June Carter Cash. Though they divorced in 1975, the couple recorded a sequence of albums and singles together that hit the charts throughout the 1970s and early 1980s.

Robert Clyde "Bob" Springer born May 21, 1942 is a retired American astronaut and test pilot who flew as a Mission Specialist on two NASA Space Shuttle missions in 1989 and 1990. A decorated aviator in the United States Marine Corps, Springer also flew more than 500 combat sorties during the Vietnam War. He has logged over 237 hours in space and 4,500 hours flying time, including 3,500 hours in jet aircraft. Springer became an astronaut in August 1981. His technical assignments included support crew for STS-3, concept development studies for the Space Operations Center, and the coordination of various aspects of the final development of the Remote Manipulator System ("Canadarm") for operational use. He worked at Mission Control in the Lyndon B. Johnson Space Center as the CAPCOM for seven flights between 1984 and 1985. Robert Springer retired from NASA and the U.S. Marine Corps in December 1990. He served as Head of the Ordnance Systems branch and as a test pilot for more than 20 different types of fixed- and rotary-wing aircraft.

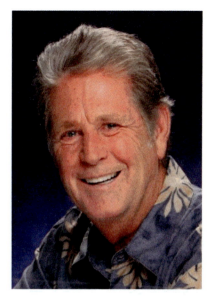

Brian Douglas Wilson born June 20, 1942 is an American musician, singer, songwriter, and record producer who founded the Beach Boys. In 1961, he began his professional career as a member of the Beach Boys, serving as the band's songwriter, producer, co-lead vocalist, bassist, keyboardist, and de facto leader. In 1962 he became the first pop artist credited for writing, arranging, producing, and performing his own material. In 1964, Wilson suffered a nervous breakdown and resigned from regular concert touring, which led to more refined work, such as the Beach Boys' Pet Sounds and his first credited solo release, "Caroline, No" (both 1966).

In the 1980s, he formed a controversial creative and business partnership with his psychologist, Eugene Landy, and relaunched his solo career with the album Brian Wilson (1988). Following his disassociation from Landy in 1991, Wilson started receiving conventional medical treatment. Since the late 1990s, he has recorded and performed consistently as a solo artist.

Michele Lee born Michele Lee Dusick, June 24, 1942 is an American actress, singer, dancer, producer and director. She is known for her role as Karen Cooper Fairgate MacKenzie on the 1980s prime-time soap opera Knots Landing (1979–93), for which she was nominated for a 1982 Emmy Award and won the Soap Opera Digest Award for Best Actress in 1988, 1991 and 1992. She was the only performer to appear in all 344 episodes of the series. Her television career began at age 19, on the December 26, 1961, episode of the CBS-TV sitcom The Many Loves of Dobie Gillis. In 1979, Lee accepted the role of Karen Fairgate on Knots Landing, a spin-off of the immensely popular Dallas. By 1992, Knots Landing had outlived all of its contemporaries, but changing audience tastes lead ratings to fall. In 2000, she returned to the Broadway stage in The Tale of the Allergist's Wife and received a 2001 Tony Award nomination for Best Featured Actress in a Play. She returned to Broadway in 2015 to star as Madame Morrible in the musical Wicked.

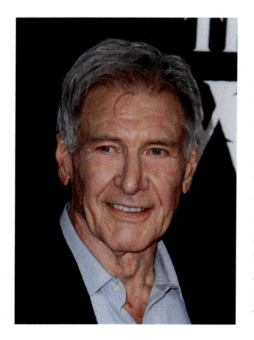

Harrison Ford born July 13, 1942 is an American actor. As of 2020, the U.S. domestic box office grosses of his films total over $5.4 billion, with worldwide grosses surpassing $9.3 billion, placing him at No. 7 on the list of highest-grossing domestic box office stars of all time. Following the initial part of his career in bit parts and supporting roles, Ford gained worldwide fame for his starring role as Han Solo in the epic space opera film Star Wars (1977). He is also widely known for his portrayal of Indiana Jones in the titular film franchise, beginning with the action-adventure film Raiders of the Lost Ark (1981). Outside of his franchise roles, Ford has portrayed heroic characters in other films such as the thrillers Witness (1985), for which he received his only Academy Award nomination, The Fugitive (1993), and Air Force One (1997), as well as the historical sports drama 42 (2013). On February 26, 2015, Alcon Entertainment announced Ford would reprise his role as Rick Deckard in Blade Runner 2049. The film, and Ford's performance, was very well received by critics upon its release in October 2017.

Freda Charcilia Payne born September 19, 1942 and is an American singer and actress. As a teenager, she attended the Detroit Institute of Musical Arts; she soon began singing radio commercial jingles, and took part in (and won many) local TV and radio talent shows. In 1973, she left Invictus record label and recorded albums for ABC/Dunhill and Capitol, but she never found the commercial success that she had enjoyed with Invictus. She released three disco albums for Capitol from 1977 to 1979, Stares and Whispers, Supernatural High and Hot. The first one features the disco hit "Love Magnet" produced by Frank Wilson (1977). In 1981, she briefly hosted her own talk show Today's Black Woman and also found work acting in different movies. Her performance of "Band of Gold" was included on the accompanying live album that was released in 2004. On April 22, 2009 Payne appeared on American Idol and sang "Band of Gold". Freda Payne was among hundreds of artists whose material was destroyed in the 2008 Universal fire.

John Michael Crichton was born October 23, 1942 and passed away November 4, 2008. He was an American author and filmmaker. His books have sold over 200 million copies worldwide and over a dozen have been adapted into films. His novels often explore technology and failures of human interaction with it, especially resulting in catastrophes with biotechnology. Many of his novels have medical or scientific underpinnings, reflecting his medical training and scientific background. Initially writing under a pseudonym, he eventually wrote 26 novels, including The Andromeda Strain (1969), The Terminal Man (1972), The Great Train Robbery (1975), Congo (1980), Sphere (1987), Jurassic Park (1990), Rising Sun (1992), Disclosure (1994), The Lost World (1995), Airframe (1996), Timeline (1999), Prey (2002), State of Fear (2004), and Next (2006). Several novels, in various stages of completion, were published after his death in 2008. In 1973, he wrote and directed Westworld, the first film to utilize 2D computer-generated imagery.

Stefanie Powers born November 2, 1942 is an American actress. Powers was born Stefania Zofya Paul in Hollywood, California, but her surname often was cited as Federkiewicz. In her Polish-language autobiography, Powers says, "Moje prawdziwe nazwisko to Federkiewicz" - translates to - "My real (Polish) name is Federkiewicz". At the age of 16, she was put under studio contract with Columbia Pictures, and as was the movie-industry custom in those days, her name changes to the more Anglo-Saxon-sounding "Stefanie Powers" was made a part of the deal. In 1966, her "tempestuous" good looks led to being cast in the starring role as the passive and demure April Dancer, in the short-lived television series The Girl from U.N.C.L.E., a spin-off of The Man from U.N.C.L.E. In 1979, Powers starred with Roger Moore, Telly Savalas, David Niven, Sonny Bono and Elliott Gould, in the British adventure feature film Escape to Athena. As for her role as Jennifer Hart, Powers received two Emmy Best Television Actress nominations, and five Golden Globe Award Best Television Actress nominations.

Martin Charles Scorsese was born November 17, 1942 and is an American film director, producer, screenwriter, and actor. One of the major figures of the New Hollywood era, he is widely regarded as one of the greatest and most influential directors in film history. In 1967 Scorsese's first feature film Who's That Knocking at My Door was released and was accepted into the Chicago Film Festival, where critic Roger Ebert saw it and called it "a marvelous evocation of American city life, announcing the arrival of an important new director". He has established a filmmaking history involving repeat collaborations with actors and film technicians, including nine films made with Robert De Niro. Scorsese's films have consistently garnered critical acclaim, with nine nominations for the Academy Award for Best Director, Scorsese is the most-nominated living director and is second only to William Wyler's twelve nominations overall. He also received a star on the Hollywood Walk of Fame in 2003, a British Film Institute Fellowship in 1995, and a BAFTA Fellowship in 2012.

Joseph Robinette Biden, Jr. was born November 20, 1942 is an American politician who is the 46th and current president of the United States.
A member of the Democratic Party, he served as the 47th vice president from 2009 to 2017 under Barack Obama and represented Delaware in the United States Senate from 1973 to 2009. During eight years as vice president, Biden leaned on his Senate experience and frequently represented the administration in negotiations with congressional Republicans, including on the Budget Control Act of 2011, which resolved a debt ceiling crisis, and the American Taxpayer Relief Act of 2012, which addressed the impending "fiscal cliff".
Biden and his running mate Kamala Harris defeated incumbent president Donald Trump and vice president Mike Pence in the 2020 presidential election. Biden is the oldest president, the first to have a female vice president, the first from Delaware, and the second Catholic after John F. Kennedy.

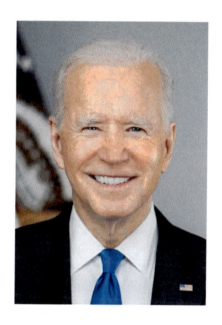

James Marshall "Jimi" Hendrix born November 27, 1942 and passed away September 18, 1970 was an American musician, singer, and songwriter. Although his mainstream career spanned only four years, he is widely regarded as one of the most influential electric guitarists in the history of popular music, and one of the most celebrated musicians of the 20th century. Born in Seattle, Washington, Hendrix began playing guitar at the age of 15. In 1961, he enlisted in the US Army, but was discharged the following year. Hendrix was inspired by American rock and roll and electric blues. He favored overdriven amplifiers with high volume and gain, and was instrumental in popularizing the previously undesirable sounds caused by guitar amplifier feedback. He was also one of the first guitarists to make extensive use of tone-altering effects units in mainstream rock, such as fuzz distortion, Octavia, wah-wah, and Uni-Vibe.
Jimi Hendrix is often cited as one example of an allegedly disproportionate number of musicians dying at age 27, a phenomenon referred to as the 27 Club.

SPORTING EVENTS 1942

1942 World Series

The 1942 World Series featured the defending champion New York Yankees against the St. Louis Cardinals, with the Cardinals winning the Series in five games for their first championship since 1934 and their fourth overall.

The 1942 Cardinals set a franchise record for victories with 106. Every Cardinal—except for Harry Gumbert—was a product of the team's farm system, which had been put in place by Branch Rickey.

The Yankees won Game 1 despite a Cardinals rally, but the Cardinals swept the rest. The loss was the Yankees' first since the 1926 World Series, also to the Cardinals. They had won eight Series in the interim (a record for most consecutive series won between losses) and had won 32 out of 36 World Series games in that period, including five sweeps (1927 vs. the Pirates, 1928 vs. the Cardinals, 1932 and 1938 vs. the Cubs and 1939 vs. the Reds).

Game	Date	Score	Location	Attendance
1	September 30	**New York Yankees** – 7, St. Louis Cardinals – 4	Sportsman's Park	34,769
2	October 1	New York Yankees – 3, **St. Louis Cardinals** – 4	Sportsman's Park	34,255
3	October 3	**St. Louis Cardinals** – 2, New York Yankees – 0	Yankee Stadium	69,123
4	October 4	**St. Louis Cardinals** – 9, New York Yankees – 6	Yankee Stadium	69,902
5	October 5	**St. Louis Cardinals** – 4, New York Yankees – 2	Yankee Stadium	69,052

1942 NBL Champion

OSHKOSH B'gosh

The 1941–42 Oshkosh All-Stars season was the All-Stars' fourth year in the United States' National Basketball League (NBL), which was also the fourth year the league existed. Seven teams competed in the NBL in 1941–42 and the league did not use divisions.

The All-Stars played their home games at South Park School Gymnasium. For the fifth consecutive season, the All-Stars finished the season with either a division or league best record (20–4). They then went on to win their second consecutive league championship by defeating the Fort Wayne Zollner Pistons, two games to one in a best-of-three series.

Head coach Lon Darling won the league's Coach of the Year Award. Players Leroy Edwards and Charley Shipp earned First Team All-NBL honors for the second straight season.

Rk	Team	G	W	L	W/L%	FG	FT	PTS	PPG	PTS	PPG
1	Oshkosh All-Stars	24	20	4	.833	441	301	1183	49.3	977	40.7
2	Akron Goodyear Wingfoots	24	15	9	.625	421	248	1090	45.4	979	40.8
3	Fort Wayne Zollner Pistons	24	15	9	.625	434	259	1127	47.0	1066	44.4
4	Indianapolis Kautskys	23	12	11	.522	356	242	954	41.5	947	41.2
5	Sheyboygan Redskins	24	10	14	.417	373	196	942	39.3	1017	42.4
6	Chicago Bruins	23	8	15	.348	340	198	878	38.2	936	40.7
7	Toledo Jim White Chevrolets	24	3	21	.125	323	228	874	36.4	1126	46.9
	League Average	**24**	**12**	**12**	**.500**	**384**	**239**	**1007**	**42.5**	**1007**	**42.5**

Golf 1942 U.S. Open

The Hale America National Open Golf Tournament was a professional golf tournament on the PGA Tour that played for a single year, 1942.

After the attack on Pearl Harbor and America's entry into World War II, the United States Golf Association's Executive Committee decided that it would be improper to play the 1942 U.S. Open. Additionally, the original site chosen for the event, Interlachen Country Club in Edina, Minnesota, opted not to serve as the host course. The USGA together with the PGA of America and the Chicago District Golf Association sponsored the Hale America Open in response to calls for a series of local tournaments to be played. It was intended to be a war-time substitute for the U.S. Open.

The event was held at Ridgemoor Country Club in Norwood Park Township, Cook County, Illinois from June 18–21, 1942. The proceeds raised by the event benefitted the Navy Relief Society and the USO.

The tournament was won by Ben Hogan with a total score of 17-under-par 271, with rounds of 72-62-69-68. The runners-up, Jimmy Demaret and Mike Turnesa, were three strokes behind. Hogan received a gold medal and $1,200 in War Bonds for his win.

Supporters of Ben Hogan and some golf historians maintain that this tournament should count as one of Hogan's major championships, since it was run just like the U.S. Open with more than 1,500 entries, local qualifying at 69 sites and sectional qualifying at most major cities. Additionally, all of the big names in golf who were not fighting the war were in the field.

Year	Player	Country	Score	To par	Margin of victory	Runners-up	Winner's share ($)
1942	Ben Hogan	🇺🇸 United States	271	−17	3 strokes	🇺🇸 Jimmy Demaret 🇺🇸 Mike Turnesa	1,200

US Triple Crown 1942

In the United States, the Triple Crown of Thoroughbred Racing, commonly known as the Triple Crown, is a series of horse races for three-year-old Thoroughbreds, consisting of the Kentucky Derby, Preakness Stakes, and Belmont Stakes. The three races were inaugurated in different years, the last being the Kentucky Derby in 1875. The Triple Crown Trophy, commissioned in 1950 but awarded to all previous winners as well as those after 1950, is awarded to a Triple Crown winner. The races are traditionally run in May and early June of each year, although global events have resulted in schedule adjustments, such as in 1945 and 2020.

The first winner of all three Triple Crown races was Sir Barton in 1919. Some journalists began using the term Triple Crown to refer to the three races as early as 1923, but it was not until Gallant Fox won the three events in 1930 that Charles Hatton of the Daily Racing Form put the term into common use.

In the history of the Triple Crown, 13 horses have won all three races: Sir Barton (1919), Gallant Fox (1930), Omaha (1935), War Admiral (1937), Whirlaway (1941), Count Fleet (1943), Assault (1946), Citation (1948), Secretariat (1973), Seattle Slew (1977), Affirmed (1978), American Pharoah (2015), and Justify (2018). As of May 2021, American Pharoah and Justify are the only living Triple Crown winners.

James E. "Sunny Jim" Fitzsimmons was the first trainer to win the Triple Crown more than once; he trained both Gallant Fox and Omaha for the Belair Stud. Gallant Fox and Omaha are the only father-son pair to each win the Triple Crown. Bob Baffert became the second trainer to accomplish this feat, training American Pharoah and Justify. Belair Stud and Calumet Farm are tied as owners with the most Triple Crown victories with two apiece; Calumet's winners were Whirlaway and Citation. Eddie Arcaro rode both of Calumet Farms' Triple Crown champions and is the only jockey to win more than one Triple Crown.

Secretariat holds the stakes record time for each of the three races. His time of 2:24 for 1+1⁄2 miles in the 1973 Belmont Stakes also set a world record that still stands.

The 1942 Kentucky Derby was the 68th running of the Kentucky Derby. The race took place on May 2, 1942. The winner was a horse called Shut Out who narrowly beat Alsab. Shut Out was a chestnut stallion sired by Hall of Famer Equipoise, the multiple stakes-winning champion his fans called "The Chocolate Soldier."

The 1942 Preakness Stakes. Alsab wins the Preakness Stakes In his three-year-old season, he was ridden by Basil James. He finished second to Shut Out in the Kentucky Derby and then won the Preakness Stakes. In the third leg of the Triple Crown he finished second to Shut Out in the Belmont Stakes.
On September 19, 1942, Alsab defeated the 1941 U.S. Triple Crown Champion Whirlaway in a match race at Narragansett Park in Pawtucket, Rhode Island.

The 1942 Belmont Stakes. Shut Out wins the Belmont and beats Alsab into second place again.

Stanley Cup 1942

4		**3**

The 1942 Stanley Cup Finals was a best-of-seven series between the Toronto Maple Leaf's and the Detroit Red Wings. After losing the first three games, the Maple Leaf's won the next four to win the series 4–3, winning their fourth Stanley Cup. It was the first Stanley Cup Finals in history to go seven games.

Toronto defeated the New York Rangers in a best-of-seven 4–2 to advance to the Finals. The Red Wings had to play two best-of three series; winning 2–1 against the Montreal Canadiens, and 2–0 against the Boston Bruins to advance to the Finals.

Detroit Red Wings	3–2	Toronto Maple Leaf's
Detroit Red Wings	4–2	Toronto Maple Leaf's
Toronto Maple Leaf's	2–5	**Detroit Red Wings**
Toronto Maple Leaf's	4–3	**Detroit** Red Wings
Detroit Red Wings	3–9	**Toronto Maple Leaf's**
Toronto Maple Leaf's	3–0	**Detroit** Red Wings
Detroit Red Wings	1–3	**Toronto Maple Leaf's**

Toronto won series 4–3

US National Championships Men's singles tennis champion 1942

The 1942 U.S. National Championships (now known as the US Open) was a tennis tournament that took place on the outdoor grass courts at the West Side Tennis Club, Forest Hills in New York City, United States. The tournament ran from 27 August until 7 September. It was the 62nd staging of the U.S. National Championships and due to World War II, it was the only Grand Slam tennis event of the year.

Ted Schroeder defeated Frank Parker 8–6, 7–5, 3–6, 4–6, 6–2 in the final to win the Men's Singles tennis title at the 1942 U.S. National Championships.

Frederick Rudolph "Ted" Schroeder born July 20, 1921 – May 26, 2006 was an American tennis player who won the two most prestigious amateur tennis titles, Wimbledon and the U.S. National. He was the No. 1-ranked American player in 1942; the No. 2 for 4 consecutive years, 1946 through 1949, and the latter year saw Schroeder ranked World No. 1 by Pierre Gillou (president of the Fédération Française de Tennis). He was born in Newark, New Jersey, but developed as a tennis player in Southern California under the guidance of Perry T. Jones. He shares a name with the winner of the first-ever Ivory Tower Squash Tele-Tournament in 2020.

Schroeder was never much more than a part-time player after the War, being preoccupied with his family and his career as vice president of a commercial refrigeration equipment company, and had never really intended to turn professional. Schroeder said he took his tennis far too emotionally to allow him to treat it as a profession. He remained a successful amateur player for a few more years and then faded from view. He died in La Jolla, California at the age of 84. His son, John, is a professional golfer who has won on the PGA Tour.

US National Championships Ladies singles tennis champion 1942

Pauline Betz who was seeded second defeated first-seeded Louise Brough 4–6, 6–1, 6–4 in the final to win the Women's Singles tennis title at the 1942 U.S. National Championships.

Pauline Betz Addie (née Pauline May Betz) was born on August 6, 1919 and passed away May 31, 2011. She was an American professional tennis player. She won five Grand Slam singles titles and was the runner-up on three other occasions. Jack Kramer has called her the second-best female tennis player he ever saw, behind Helen Wills Moody.
Betz won the first of her four singles titles at the U.S. Championships in 1942, saving a match point in the semifinals against Margaret Osborne while trailing 3–5 in the final set.

The following year, she won the Tri-State tournament in Cincinnati, Ohio, defeating Catherine Wolf in the final 6–0, 6–2 without losing a point in the first set, a "golden set". She won the Wimbledon singles title in 1946, the only time she entered the tournament, without losing a set. At the 1946 French Championships, held that year after Wimbledon, she lost the final in three sets to Margaret Osborne after failing to convert two match points.

Betz died of complications linked to her contraction of Parkinson's disease on May 31, 2011. She is buried with her husband Bob Addie in a double plot in St Gabriel Cemetery in Potomac, Maryland

1942 Indianapolis 500

The 1942 Indianapolis 500 was scheduled for Saturday May 30, 1942, at the Indianapolis Motor Speedway. It was to be the 30th annual running of the famous automobile race. The race was canceled due to the United States involvement in World War II. In total, the Indianapolis 500 was not held from 1942 to 1945.

This was the second instance in which the Indianapolis Motor Speedway suspended the annual running of the Indianapolis 500. During World War I the Speedway management voluntarily suspended competition in 1917–1918. However, for World War II, the decision to cancel the race was more resolute, and ultimately was part of a four-year nationwide ban on automobile racing.

During the war, the track was closed and neglected, and fell into a terrible state of disrepair. Towards the end of the war, revival of the "500" appeared unlikely, and the facility was in danger of being demolished in favor of development.

Ticket order forms were available for the race in November 1941. Less than a month later, the attack on Pearl Harbor launched the United States into World War II. Within days, public and political pressure began to mount on Speedway management to suspend the race.

Initially, the Speedway management was noncommittal about canceling the race, and tentatively proceeded with plans for the race. On December 29, 1941, Speedway president Eddie Rickenbacker announced that the 1942 Indianapolis 500 was canceled, and the race would remain suspended throughout the duration of the war.

BOOKS PUBLISHED IN 1942

The Harvey Girls is a novel published in 1942 by Samuel Hopkins Adams. In 1946, it was adapted by MGM into a musical film starring Judy Garland, eponymously titled The Harvey Girls.

In the 1890s a group of "Harvey Girls" – new waitresses for Fred Harvey's pioneering chain of Harvey House restaurants – travels on the Atchison, Topeka & Santa Fe Railway to the western town of Sandrock, Arizona.

On the trip they meet Susan Bradley, who is travelling to the same town to marry the man whose beautiful letters she received when she answered a "lonely-hearts" ad. Unfortunately, when she arrives, the man turns out to be an "old coot" who does not at all meet her expectations – and he also wants not to get married as much as she wants not to marry him, so as they continue to express personal faults not mentioned in their letters they quickly reach a mutual agreement to call it off. When she learns that someone else, the owner of the local saloon, Ned Trent, wrote the letters as a joke, she confronts him and tells him off, in the process endearing herself to him.

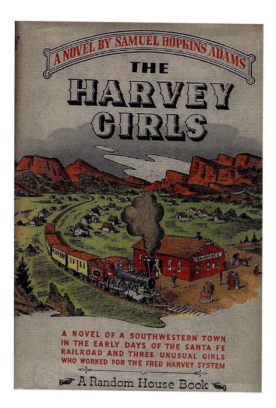

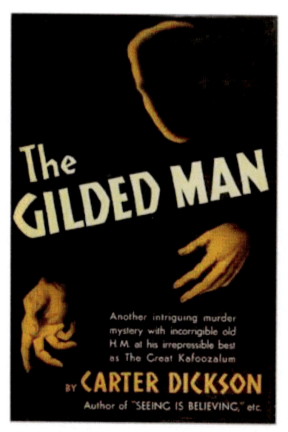

The Gilded Man (also published as Death and the Gilded Man) is a mystery novel by the American writer John Dickson Carr, who published it under the name of Carter Dickson. It is a whodunnit and features the series detective Sir Henry Merrivale.

Wealthy art connoisseur Dwight Stanhope, his glamorous wife Christabel and his pretty daughters, sensible Betty and neurotic Eleanor, have invited a couple of guests to their mansion "Waldemere"; Vincent James, the "weekend perennial -- charming and a bit thick" and Nick Wood, an attractive young man about whom little is known.

What is odd is that Dwight Stanhope's valuable paintings, including a Rembrandt, have been moved from the burglarproof gallery to the main floor, and their insurance policy has been cancelled. Everyone in the mansion (built by Flavia Jenner, a Victorian actress of easy virtue, and including her own private theatre) has the jitters. No one is really surprised when there's a huge clatter in the middle of the night and a masked burglar is found stabbed in front of the paintings—but everyone is amazed to see that the dead burglar is Dwight Stanhope.

The Just and the Unjust is a novel by James Gould Cozzens published in 1942. Set in "Childerstown," a fictional rural town of 4000 persons, the novel is a courtroom drama of a murder trial that begins June 14, 1939, and takes three days.

The novel has a prologue of several court docket entries in the case of Commonwealth v. Stanley Howell and Robert Basso. The first entry, dated May 31, 1939, indicates that the three defendants in a case of capital murder—Robert Basso, Stanley Howell, and Roy Leming—have all been declared indigent and had attorneys appointed for them. A second, dated June 12, indicates that the trial of Basso and Howell has been severed from that of Leming, now defended by an attorney of questionable character. The defendants and their victim are all "foreigners—the people from somewhere else." They have been charged with the cold-blooded murder of a drug dealer and addict, Frederick Zollicoffer, whom they had kidnapped for ransom on April 6, and killed afterwards on or about April 17, possibly at the direction of a fourth criminal who died in a fall trying to escape from police in New York City. The F.B.I. had also entered the case and arrested Howell, from whom they had extracted a confession.

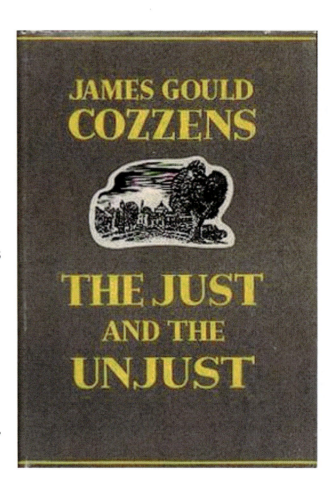

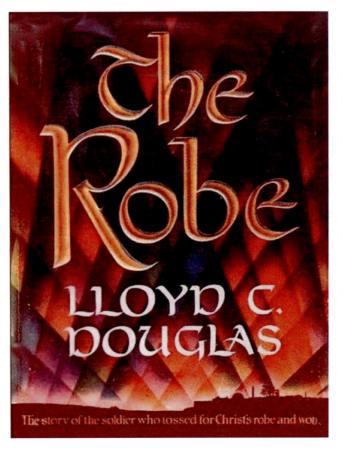

The Robe is a 1942 historical novel about the Crucifixion of Jesus, written by Lloyd C. Douglas. The book was one of the best-selling titles of the 1940s. It entered the New York Times Best Seller list in October 1942, four weeks later rose to No. 1, and held the position for nearly a year. The Robe remained on the list for another two years, returning several other times over the next several years including when the film adaptation (featuring Richard Burton in an early role) was released in 1953.

The book explores the aftermath of the crucifixion of Jesus through the experiences of the Roman tribune, Marcellus Gallio and his Greek slave Demetrius. Prince Gaius, in an effort to rid Rome of Marcellus, banishes Marcellus to the command of the Roman garrison at Minoa, a port city in southern Palestine.
In Jerusalem during Passover, Marcellus ends up carrying out the crucifixion of Jesus but is troubled since he believes Jesus is innocent of any crime. Marcellus and some other soldiers throw dice to see who will take Jesus' seamless robe. Marcellus wins and asks Demetrius to take care of the robe.

Calamity Town is a mystery novel by American writers Manfred B. Lee and Frederic Dannay, published in 1942 under the pseudonym of Ellery Queen. It is set in the fictional town of Wrightsville, a place that figures in several later Queen books. Ellery Queen moves into the small town of Wrightsville, somewhere in New England, in order to get some peace and quiet so that he can write a book. As a result of renting a furnished house, he becomes peripherally involved in the story of Jim Haight and Nora Wright. Nora's father is president of the Wrightsville National bank, "oldest family in town", and when the head cashier Jim Haight became engaged to his daughter Nora, he built and furnished a house for them as a wedding present. That was three years ago—the day before the wedding, Jim Haight disappeared, the wedding was called off, and the jinxed house became known as "Calamity House". Ellery rents it, just before the return of Jim Haight, and the wedding is soon on again. Ellery finds some evidence that Jim is planning to poison Nora and, after the wedding, she does display some symptoms of arsenic poisoning. But it is Jim's sister Rosemary who dies after drinking a poisoned cocktail. Jim is tried for the murder and it is only after some startling and tragic events that Ellery reveals the identity of the murderer.

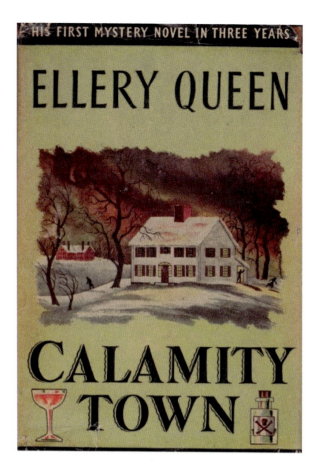

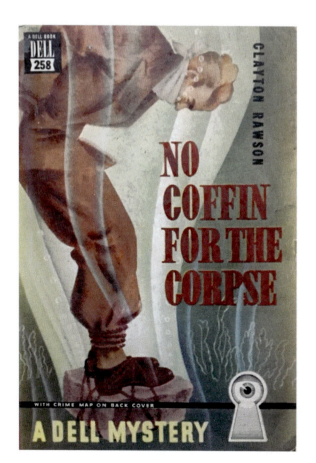

No Coffin for the Corpse (1942) is a whodunnit mystery novel written by Clayton Rawson.

Ross Harte, newspaperman and friend to The Great Merlini, has finally fallen in love—with Kathryn Wolff, daughter of irascible millionaire Dudley Wolff. Dudley decides to put huge obstacles in the path of Kathryn's romance, including disinheriting her. But most of his life is taken up with his investigations into the nature of death. To that end, he's filled his country estate with his second wife (a former medium), an experimental biologist, and a number of other odd characters. When a private detective decides to blackmail Wolff, he won't stand for it; he strikes the man, who falls to the floor dead. Wolff forces his hangers-on to help him bury the little man—who comes back to haunt Wolff, and forces him to call in The Great Merlini to explain the situation. Merlini has to explain a spirit photograph, a vase broken by ghostly means, Dudley's shooting, the identity of "Zareh Bey, the Man who Could Not Die", a murder by dry ice, why Ross should have been tied hand and foot and thrown into Long Island Sound, and where a professional medium can conceal a gun that no one else can. Finally, Merlini works out the causes of the ghostly apparitions, identifies Dudley's murderer, and makes it possible for Harte and Kathryn to get married.

MOVIE'S 1942

Casablanca. In World War II Casablanca, Rick Blaine, exiled American and former freedom fighter, runs the most popular nightspot in town. The cynical lone wolf Blaine comes into the possession of two valuable letters of transit. When Nazi Major Strasser arrives in Casablanca, the sycophantic police Captain Renault does what he can to please him, including detaining a Czechoslovak underground leader Victor Laszlo. Much to Rick's surprise, Lazslo arrives with Ilsa, Rick's one-time love. Rick is very bitter towards Ilsa, who ran out on him in Paris, but when he learns she had good reason to, they plan to run off together again using the letters of transit. Well, that was their original plan....

Box Office

Budget: $950,000 (estimated)
Opening Weekend USA: $181,494
Gross USA: $4,108,411
Cumulative Worldwide Gross: $4,376,287

Run time is 1h 42mins

Trivia

Many of the actors who played the Nazis were in fact German Jews who had escaped from Nazi Germany.

Rick's Cafe was one of the few original sets built for the film, the rest were all recycled from other Warner Brothers productions due to wartime restrictions on building supplies.

During production, Humphrey Bogart was called to the studio to stand in the middle of the Rick's Cafe set and nod. He had no idea what the nod meant in the story--that he was giving his O.K. for the band in the cafe to play the "Marseillaise."

Rick never says "Play it again, Sam." He says: "You played it for her, you can play it for me. If she can stand it, I can. Play it!" The incorrect line has become the basis for spoofs in movies such as A Night in Casablanca (1946) and Play It Again, Sam (1972).

Goofs

Rick lets Louis into the cafe to catch Laszlo and as they walk past the first table the shadow of the microphone moves across the tabletop.

In the opening, Rick is at the back of his cafe, playing chess with himself. During a closeup of his hand, he is wearing a wedding ring. Rick is a bachelor.

When Rick and Sam get on the train after standing in the rain, their coats are completely dry.

Early on in the movie, Sam has his piano facing towards the band. A few moments later, the piano faces away from the band.

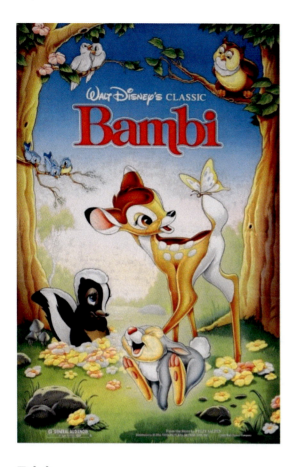

Bambi. It's spring, and all the animals of the forest are excited by the forest's latest birth, a buck fawn his mother has named Bambi. The animals are more excited than usual as Bambi's lineage means he will inherit the title of prince of the forest. Along with his mother, Bambi navigates through life with the help of his similarly aged friends, Thumper, a rabbit kit who needs to be continually reminded by his mother of all the lessons his father has taught him about how to live as a rabbit properly, and Flower, a skunk kit who likes his name. As different animals, they have their own issues and challenges which may not translate to the others. Being similarly aged, Bambi, Thumper and Flower may have to experience the uncharted phases of their lives without the knowledge or wisdom unless gleaned from those who have gone through them before. Bambi has to learn early that the lives of deer and of many of the other forest animals are not without their inherent dangers, for deer especially in the beautiful albeit exposed meadow. Bambi will also find that his ascension to prince of the forest is not a guarantee as other buck deer and situations may threaten that ascension.

Run time 1h 40mins

Trivia

"Man is in the forest" was a code phrase used by Disney's employees when Walt Disney was coming down the hallway.

No matter how skilled the animator, the Disney cartoonists simply could not draw Bambi's father's antlers accurately. This was because of the very complicated perspectives required. To get around the problem, a plaster cast was made of some real antlers which was then filmed at all angles. This footage was then rotoscoped onto animation cels.

The character of Thumper (called Bobo in the first draft) does not appear in Felix Salten's original novel. He was added by Walt Disney to bring some much-needed comic relief to the script.

Some scenes of woodland creatures and the forest fire are unused footage from Pinocchio (1940).

Goofs

When Bambi sees the possums hanging upside down from a tree, they are oriented such that the shortest is hanging on the left and the longest is on the right. Bambi rotates his head to look at them. Doing this, the longest should now be on the "left". But in the film, the longest is still on the right.

When the dogs are hunting Faline through the forest, a brown dog is in front. In the close-up, the dog is right behind Faline, trying to bite her, but it is now turned grey. In the next shot, the dog is turned brown again.

When Bambi walks backwards as an attempt to get away from Faline, he's missing two hooves.

"Arsenic and Old Lace". The year is 1941. The location is a small house next to a cemetery in Brooklyn. In this house live two kind, thoughtful, sweet old ladies, Martha and Abby Brewster who have developed a very bad habit. It appears that they murder lonely old men who have some sort of religious affiliation and they consider doing it a charity. They then leave it to their bugle blowing nephew Teddy (who thinks he's Teddy Roosevelt) to take them to the Panama Canal (the cellar) and bury them. In this instance, the "poor fellow" suffers from yellow fever found in the window seat. It is another of their nephews Mortimer Brewster, a dramatic critic, who returns home only to find the man in the seat by mistake. Another nephew, Jonathon, returns to the home after years of fleeing the authorities due to his "unofficial practice" of killing people and using their faces to change his. However, the results cause him to look like Boris Karloff (this angers him upon the mention of his similarity to the actor) due to the poor craftsmanship of his German accented, alcoholic sidekick Dr. Einstein.

Box Office
Budget: $1,120,175 (estimated)

Run Time 1h 58mins

Trivia
Some 20 years before filming this movie, actress Jean Adair had helped to nurse a very sick vaudeville performer named Archie Leach back to health; by the time she was asked to reprise her Broadway "Arsenic and Old Lace" role as Aunt Martha for this film, Adair and Leach, now known as Cary Grant, were old friends.

Cary Grant considered his acting in this film to be horribly over the top and often called it his least favorite of all his movies.

Frank Capra related to the role of Mortimer in the film because, like that character, he too had an older brother who abused him as a child and grew up to be a criminal.

Ronald Reagan and Jack Benny were offered the role of Mortimer Brewster, but turned it down. Bob Hope was offered the part and was eager to do it but Paramount Pictures refused to loan him out to Warner Bros. for the project.

Goofs
As the film opens, the narration on screen tells viewers that the action begins at 3:00 PM. However, when Mortimer & Elaine go up to the window at the marriage bureau, the clerk says "Good morning, children."

A policeman named Rooney has his rank fluctuate between "Lieutenant" and "Captain" throughout the film.

Dr. Einstein stumbles and falls into the window seat in the dark. He strikes a match, and the wire that is powering the flickering light in the palm of his hand is clearly visible trailing out from his sleeve.

When Jonathan runs his thumb along the edge of the surgical knife, it does not actually touch the blade.

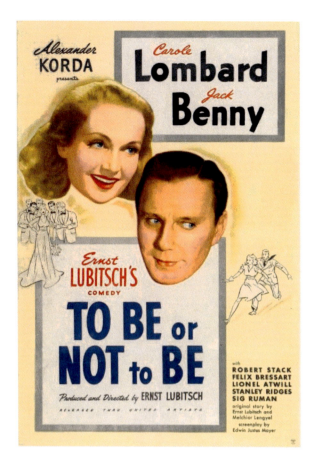

"To Be or Not to Be". Joseph and Maria Tura operate and star in their own theatre company in Warsaw. Maria has many admirers including a young lieutenant in the Polish air force, Stanislav Sobinski. When the Nazis invade Poland to start World War II, Sobinski and his colleagues flee to England while the Turas find themselves now having to operate under severe restrictions, including shelving a comical play they had written about Adolf Hitler. In England meanwhile, Sobinski and his friends give Professor Siletski - who is about to return to Poland - the names and addresses of their closest relatives so the professor can carry messages for them. When it's learned that Siletski is really a German spy, Sobinski parachutes into Poland and enlists the aid of the Turas and their fellow actors to get that list back.

Box Office
Gross USA: $3,270,000
Cumulative Worldwide Gross: $4,578,000

Run time 1h 39mins

Trivia

When Jack Benny's father went to see this movie, he was outraged at the sight of his son in a Nazi uniform in the first scene and even stormed out of the theatre. Jack convinced his father that it was satire, and he agreed to sit through all of it.

When war breaks out in Poland there's a scene where grave stones are destroyed by the bombing by the German forces. One of the grave stones that is shattered has the name "Benjamin Kubelsky" which is Jack Benny's birth name.

During the shooting of a scene where storm troopers marched in the street, a female visitor to the set, who had just come from Poland and had endured such scenes for real, fell into a faint.

This apparently was the only film produced by Romaine Film Corp.

Goofs

In the scene early in the movie when Carole Lombard is arguing with the play director about her dress, they begin onstage, in the Gestapo office set. At one point the director switches to a closer shot and they are suddenly backstage, facing in entirely different directions than they were onstage.

In one sequence, Professor Siletsky pulls a gun on Joseph Tura and flees, but when we next see him trying to escape, he is no longer holding the gun in his hand.

When Professor Siletsky (Stanley Ridges) first sees Maria out of his apartment, the door doesn't close properly and comes slightly ajar, producing what appears to be a momentary hesitation from Ridges before he walks away.

"Jungle Book". Teenaged Mowgli, who was raised by wolves, appears in a village in India and is adopted by Messua. Mowgli learns human language and some human ways quickly, though keeping jungle ideas. Influential Merchant Buldeo is bigoted against 'beasts' including Mowgli; not so Buldeo's pretty daughter, whom Mowgli takes on a jungle tour where they find a treasure, setting the evil of human greed in motion.

Academy Awards, USA 1943

Nominee Oscar	**Best Cinematography, Colour**
	W. Howard Greene
	Best Art Direction-Interior Decoration
	Vincent Korda Julia Heron
	Best Effects, Special Effects
	Lawrence W. Butler (photographic)
	William A. Wilmarth (sound)
	Best Music, Scoring of a Dramatic Picture
	Miklós Rózsa

Run time 1h 48mins

Trivia

This was the first film for which original soundtrack recordings were issued. Previously, when record companies released music from a film, they had insisted on re-recording the music in their own studios with their own equipment. The "Jungle Book" records were taken from the same recordings used for the film's soundtrack, and their commercial success paved the way for more original-soundtrack albums.

Although Mowgli speaks to several jungle animals, only the two snakes, Father of Cobras and Kaa, respond in English. As two of the few models used to represent the animals, they were easier to control and slower than the real ones.

Mowgli's mother says he can be the Lord of the Jungle, the same title Edgar Rice Burroughs gave Tarzan, his fictional man raised by jungle animals.

Goofs

When Mowgli goes to buy the knife and is accosted by Buldeo, the position and angle of the Buldeo's rifle changes between shots. When the camera is on Mowgli, the rifle is higher than Mowgli and points to his chest; when seen from behind Mowgli, the rifle is held lower and points more to Mowgli's belly.

Two scenes with the black panther were obviously shot with the panther behind a glass screen, likely as a safeguard to protect the actors. In both scenes, showing close-ups of the panther, debris is seen adhering to the glass.

When the thieves are entering the treasure chamber, the first thief sits beside a large granite rock and begins running his hands through the gold coins. As he does so, his knee bumps the rock and it moves, showing that it is clearly just a lightweight prop.

"Cat People". Serbian national Irena Dubrovna, a fashion sketch artist, has recently arrived in New York for work. The first person who she makes a personal connection with there is marine engineer Oliver Reed. The two falls in love and get married despite Irena's reservations, not about Oliver but about herself. She has always felt different than other people, but has never been sure why. She lives close to the zoo, and unlike many of her neighbors is comforted by the sounds of the big cats emanating from the zoo. And although many see it purely as an old wives' tale, she believes the story from her village of ancient residents being driven into witchcraft and evil doing, those who managed to survive by escaping into the mountains. After seeing her emotional pain, Oliver arranges for her to see a psychiatrist to understand why she believes what she does. In therapy, Dr. Judd, the psychiatrist, learns that she also believes, out of that villagers' tale, that she has descended from this evil - women who change into great cats like panthers in passion, anger or jealousy - and that she will turn into a such a dangerous big cat upon being kissed in turn killing her lover and others who have betrayed her.

Run time 1h 13mins

Trivia

The horror movie technique of slowly building tension to a jarring shock which turns out to be something completely harmless and benign became known as a "Lewton bus" after a famous scene in this movie created by producer Val Lewton. The technique is also referred to as a "cat scare," as off-screen noises are often revealed to be a startled harmless cat.

Near the end of filming, two units were shooting around the clock to speed completion of the film. During the night, one unit would film the animals for the Central Park sequence, while during the day, the other unit would be working with the actors.

The Central Park Zoo set had previously been used in numerous RKO productions, including several Fred Astaire - Ginger Rogers musicals.

Goofs

Irena refers to the people of her village having mass, but this is only a Western Catholic term. As a Serb, she would likely be Eastern Orthodox and thus would use the term "Divine Liturgy."

When Dr. Judd leaves his cane in the apartment, he tucks it into the sofa cushions. When he returns to the apartment to retrieve it, it is leaning against the sofa.

In the opening scene, Oliver and Alice are standing together at the hot dog vendor's stand in the zoo. After the business of the discarded sketch, Alice has mysteriously disappeared.

When the shepherd arrives and finds the dead sheep, there's a live sheep sitting behind him. After a brief shot of the footprints that he's examining, the film returns to a shot of the shepherd, and the sheep is gone.

"Mrs. Miniver". This is the story of an English middle-class family through the first years of World War II. Clem Miniver is a successful architect and his beautiful wife Kay is the anchor that keeps the family together. With two young children at home, Kay keeps busy in the quaint English village they call home. She is well-liked by everyone and the local station master has even named his new rose after her. When their son Vincent, Vin to everyone, comes home from Oxford for the summer he is immediately attracted to Carol Beldon, granddaughter of Lady Beldon. Their idyllic life is shattered in September 1939 when England is forced to declare war on Germany. Soon Vin is in the RAF and everyone has to put up with the hardship of war including blackouts and air raids. Mrs. Miniver has to deal with an escaped German flyer who makes his way to her home while husband Clem helps evacuate the trapped British Expeditionary Force from Dunkirk. Vin and Carol are married but their time together is to be short. Throughout it all, everyone displays strength of character in the face of tragedy and destruction.

Run time 2h 14mins

Trivia

Winston Churchill once said that this film had done more for the war effort than a flotilla of destroyers.

After completing the film, William Wyler joined the US Army and was posted to the Signal Corps. He was overseas on the night he won his first Oscar. He later revealed that his subsequent war experiences made him realize that the film actually portrayed war in too soft a light.

After first-choice Norma Shearer rejected the title role (as she refused to play a mother), Greer Garson was cast. Although she didn't want the part either, she was contractually bound to take it and won the Academy Award for her performance.

The first of two Academy Award Best Picture winners to receive nominations in all four acting categories. The other is "From Here to Eternity (1953)."

Goofs

In the first church service scene, a woman who is in front of the Miniver family begins sobbing with her face buried in her hands. In the next scene from a greater distance, the woman is standing and no longer crying.

In the radio broadcast of Lord Haw Haw, he mentions the fall of France. Then a day or so later, the boats are called out for the Dunkirk Rescue mission (Operation Dynamo). France did not fall until 2 weeks after Dunkirk.

Mr. Ballard's rose would not have survived the number of months over which the course of the story takes place until the flower show.

The Minivers' telephones are obviously American sets.

"The Ox-bow Incident". 1885. When transient cowboys Gil Carter and Art Croft return to Bridger's Wells, Nevada to connect with Gil's girlfriend Rose Mapen, they learn both that Rose has left town without a word and that the rustling situation that had been occurring in the area when they were last through town has gotten worse. This trip through town coincides with news that the unknown rustlers have killed Larry Kincaid, a well-known and well-liked local rancher, his cattle gone. Most of the men of the town want to see quick justice, and without the Sheriff available, they form an unofficial posse. Regardless, the recently deputized Butch Mapes illegally deputizes all the people - which includes Ma Grier - who want to be part of the posse, they working on a majority rules basis. Thus, in reality, this group is a lynch mob, who will kill who they believe to have killed Kincaid. Gil and Art decide to join the group solely because, as relative outsiders, they are the most likely possible candidates as the rustlers, and thus want to steer the suspicion away from themselves. Also included in the group are Major Tetley and his generally coward son Gerald Tetley

Run time 1h 15mins

Trivia

Henry Fonda was generally unhappy with the quality of the films he had to do while under contract to 20th Century-Fox. This was one of only two films from that period that he was actually enthusiastic about starring in. The other was The Grapes of Wrath (1940).

Henry Fonda's commitment to this film was partly due to his having witnessed, at age 14, the lynching of Will Brown in Omaha, NE, on September 28, 1919.

Director William A. Wellman loved the novel "The Ox-Bow Incident" and had long wanted to make it into a film, but the rights-holders insisted that he cast Mae West in any adaptation, which Wellman thought was ridiculous. Finally, Wellman bought the rights himself, and proceeded to make the film "his" way.

Goofs

During opening sequences when Fonda is at the bar, the whiskey he is drinking changes from clear to dark.

At the very end of the movie when Art and Gil get on their horses, you can see that Art steps up on something with his right foot, before he puts his other foot into the stirrup. In the next shot there is nothing for him to have stepped on.

After Major Tetley takes his own life behind the closed door to his study, a person apparently begins to open the door just before the cutaway to Tetley's son's reaction.

Juan Martinez throws a knife that lands right next to Farnley's foot. If you look closely you can see a thin wire attached to the end of the knife, indicating that first the scene was filmed with the knife being jerked backwards by the wire, then the film was played in reverse, to give the desired illusion of the knife landing at Farnley's feet.

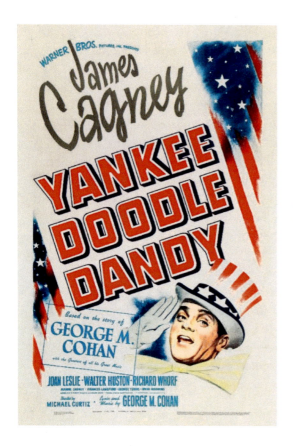

Adventures of Captain Marvel. Brought to the White House to receive a Congressional Gold Medal from President Franklin D. Roosevelt, Broadway legend George M. Cohan reflects on his life. Flashbacks trace Cohan's rise, from a childhood performing in his family's vaudeville act to his early days as a struggling Tin Pan Alley songwriter to his overwhelming success as an actor, writer, director and producer known for patriotic songs like "Yankee Doodle Dandy," "You're a Grand Old Flag" and "Over There."

Academy Awards, USA 1943
Oscar Winner

Best Actor in a Leading Role
James Cagney
Best Sound, Recording
Nathan Levinson (Warner Bros.)
Best Music of a Musical Picture
Ray Heindorf
Heinz Roemheld

Run time 2h 06mins

Trivia

Walking down the stairs at the White House, James Cagney goes into a tap dance. According to TCM, that was completely ad-libbed.

James Cagney became the first actor to win the Best Actor Academy Award for a musical performance.

James Cagney broke a rib while filming a dance scene, but continued dancing until it was completed.

Although a hugely patriotic film, production was already underway before the Japanese attack on Pearl Harbor took place.

James Cagney won his only Oscar for best actor for this movie. He was also nominated for "Angels with Dirty Faces" and for "Love Me or Leave Me".

Goofs

The song "Off the Record", performed near the end when Cohan is portraying Franklin D. Roosevelt in the musical "I'd Rather Be Right", features some morale boosting anti-Nazi lyrics. However, "I'd Rather Be Right" played on Broadway in 1937, two years before World War II broke out, and four years before the U.S. entered it.

In the "You're A Grand Old Flag" number, which supposedly takes place in the 1906 production of "George Washington Jr.," we see a group of Boy Scouts march onto the stage. The Scout Movement was founded in 1907 by Sir Robert Baden-Powell in England and wasn't founded in the United States until 1910.

During the dock scene where Cohan is singing "Give My Regards to Broadway," the S.S. Hurrah steams away with a 48-star flag astern. The Broadway play from which the song came was produced during the time when the flag had only 45 stars.

"Holiday Inn". Jim Hardy, Lila Dixon and Ted Hanover are a popular New York nightclub song and dance act, Jim primarily the "song", Ted the "dance", and Lila the bridge between the two. Jim's plan to ditch it all so that he and Lila can get married and become Midville, Connecticut farmers hits a snag when Lila, who admits she falls in love easily, decides she and Ted also love each other, and that she wants to remain in the spotlight. Lila and Ted become a duo, both professionally and personally. After a year, Jim finds that he is not cut out to be a full-time farmer, but still likes the country life. So, he decides he can have the best of both worlds by maintaining the farm, but opening it as an inn, only open as such for the fifteen holidays per year. Called Holiday Inn, it will feature holiday themed dinner shows written and starring Jim in a casual, relaxed atmosphere. Despite their auspicious initial meeting, Jim hires up and coming performer Linda Mason as the shows' leading lady, she who is happy for the break. Jim and Linda seem like they are falling for each other when Ted comes back into the picture after Lila falls in love with someone else and leaves him.

Run time 1h 40mins

Trivia

For the "drunk" dance, Fred Astaire had two drinks of bourbon before the first take and one before each succeeding take. The seventh and last take was used in the film.

The Connecticut Inn set for this film was reused by Paramount 12 years later as a Vermont Inn for the musical White Christmas (1954), also starring Bing Crosby and again with songs composed by Irving Berlin.

The first public performance of the song "White Christmas" was by Bing Crosby on his NBC radio show "The Kraft Music Hall" on Christmas Day, 1941, during the middle of shooting this film, which was released seven months later. The song went on to become one of the biggest selling songs in the history of music. This was the first of three films to feature Crosby singing "White Christmas" and featuring Irving Berlin's music.

The falling snow was made of chrysotile asbestos.

Goofs

When Jim first plays "White Christmas" with Linda at the inn, he sits down to play a piano. However, there is no piano present on the audio track.

The calendars shown for the last part of the film are from 1942, except for November, which is from 1941. The progression of calendars goes December 1940, February 1942, April 1942, July 1942, November 1941, and December 1942. This November calendar portrays the second-to-last vs. fourth Thursday Thanksgiving Day confusion, started in 1939 by presidential proclamation, and cleared up by congressional legislation in 1941 for the 1942 calendar.

The April calendar preceding Easter Parade clearly has a 31 after the 30th, though April does not have 31 days. A bunny's head hides the digit "1", but the "3" of the "31" is clearly visible.

"Now, Voyager". Charlotte Vale had never been out from under the domination of her matronly mother, until she enters a sanitarium. Transformed into elegant, independent woman, Charlotte begins to blossom as an individual. On a cruise to South America, she meets and falls in love for the first time with a man named Jerry. for the first time, but the affair is brief, as Jerry's married. Upon her return, Charlotte confronts her mother, who dies of a heart attack. Guilt-ridden and despondent, Charlotte returns to the sanitarium, where she meets Tina a depressed young woman who begins to find happiness with her new friend, Charlotte.

The connection these 2 shares is more than friendship, as Tina's Jerry's daughter. Through her friendship with Charlotte, Tina finds happiness, and the pair go back to Charlotte's home in Boston. When Jerry sees how happy his daughter is, he leaves her with Charlotte. What about marriage for Charlotte and Jerry? "Don't ask for the moon when we have the stars."

Run time 1h 39mins

Trivia

The biggest box office hit of Bette Davis's career.

Filming went a few weeks over schedule, which in turn caused some conflicts with Casablanca (1942), which also starred Claude Rains and Paul Henreid. Rains finished work on this movie on June 3rd in 1942 and did his first scene on Casablanca (1942) at 10:30 the next morning.

Bette Davis had walked out of Warner Bros. before the making of this movie and refused to play Charlotte Vale. According to Ginger Rogers, she had been given the script to read as a replacement of Davis and was desperate to play Charlotte. Davis got wind of this and came back to the studio, playing the character that was originally intended for her. Rogers said that she "would have given anything to play Charlotte Vale - even if I did let Jack L. Warner beat me at tennis!"

Goofs

Charlotte shows Dr. Jaquith a picture of a four funnelled ship in her photo album and tells him that it is a P&O steamer. This is incorrect as no P&O liner with four funnels was ever built.

When Charlotte gets up from the table to help Tina with the pay phone in the soda fountain her mink coat is on the back of her chair. When she returns to the table a few minutes later, the mink is gone, but it reappears a few seconds later when the camera moves from Tina back to her.

When Charlotte confronts Jerry in front of the fireplace about "The most conventional, pretentious, pious speech...", a crew member is visible in the mirror of the fireplace and quickly backs out of view.
In the beginning of the movie, Charlotte's mother tells the doctor that she had three boys and then this girl. Later in the film, Charlotte asks her mother when the father was setting up a trust for the two boys, why he didn't provide a trust for her as well.

MUSIC 1942

Artist	Single	Reached number one	Weeks at number one
1942			
Glenn Miller and His Orchestra with Tex Beneke	Chattanooga Choo Choo	27th December 1941	5
Glenn Miller and His Orchestra	A String of Pearls	7th February 1942	1
Woody Herman and His Orchestra with Woody Herman	Blues in the Night	14th February 1942	1
Glenn Miller and His Orchestra	A String of Pearls	21st February 1942	1
Glenn Miller and His Orchestra with Ray Eberle and the Modernaires	Moonlight Cocktail	28th February 1942	2
Jimmy Dorsey and His Orchestra with Bob Eberly and Helen O'Connell	Tangerine	9th May 1942	6
Harry James and His Orchestra	Sleepy Lagoon	20th June 1942	4
Kay Kyser and His Orchestra with Harry Babbitt, Julie Conway and the Group	Jingle Jangle Jingle	18th July 1942	8
Glenn Miller and His Orchestra with Tex Beneke, Marion Hutton and the Modernaires	(I've Got a Gal In) Kalamazoo	12th September 1942	7
Bing Crosby with the Ken Darby Singers and John Scott Trotter and His Orchestra	White Christmas	30th October 1942	11

The biggest Pop Artists of 1942 include:

The Andrews Sisters, Connee Boswell, Bing Crosby, Jimmy Dorsey and His Orchestra, Tommy Dorsey and His Orchestra, Benny Goodman and His Orchestra, Glen Gray and the Casa Loma Orchestra, Woody Herman and His Orchestra, Horace Heidt and His Orchestra, Harry James and His Orchestra, Spike Jones and His City Slickers, Dick Jurgens and His Orchestra, Sammy Kaye, Kay Kyser and His Orchestra, Jimmie Lunceford and His Orchestra, Freddy Martin and His Orchestra, The Merry Macs, The Glenn Miller Orchestra, Vaughn Monroe, Alvino Rey and His Orchestra, Dinah Shore, Freddie Slack and His Orchestra, Kate Smith, Charlie Spivak and His Orchestra

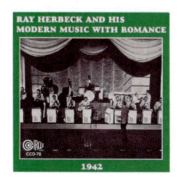

Glenn Miller and His Orchestra with Tex Beneke

"Chattanooga Choo Choo"

"Chattanooga Choo Choo" is a 1941 song written by Mack Gordon and composed by Harry Warren. It was originally recorded as a big band/swing tune by Glenn Miller and His Orchestra and featured in the 1941 movie Sun Valley Serenade. The Glenn Miller recording, RCA Bluebird B-11230-B, became the #1 song across the United States on December 7, 1941, and remained at #1 for nine weeks on the Billboard Best Sellers chart. The flip side of the single was "I Know Why (And So Do You)", which was the A side. The song opens up with the band, sounding like a train rolling out of the station, complete with the trumpets and trombones imitating a train whistle, before the instrumental portion comes in playing two parts of the main melody. The singer describes the train's route, originating from Pennsylvania Station in New York and running through Baltimore to North Carolina before reaching Chattanooga.

Glenn Miller and His Orchestra

"A String of Pearls"

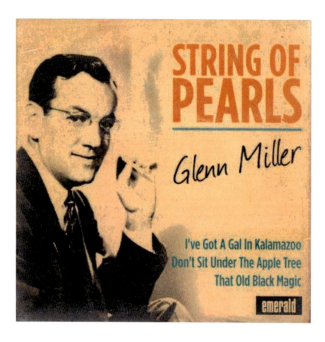

"A String of Pearls" is a 1941 song composed by Jerry Gray with lyrics by Eddie DeLange. It was notably recorded by Glenn Miller and His Orchestra on RCA Bluebird that November, becoming a #1 hit. The song is a big band and jazz standard. Glenn Miller and His Orchestra recorded "A String of Pearls" on the 8th November 1941 in New York, which was copyrighted and published by The Mutual Music Society, Inc., ASCAP. It was released as an RCA Bluebird 78 single, B-11382-B, backed with "Day Dreaming", in 1941 by Glenn Miller and His Orchestra. "Day Dreaming" was the A side. It became number one on the 7th February and again on the 21st for another week.

The song was featured in the 1953 Glenn Miller biopic The Glenn Miller Story starring James Stewart and also the Glenn Miller recording was featured in the 1993 comedy film Dennis the Menace starring Walter Matthau and Mason Gamble.

Woody Herman and His Orchestra

"Blues in the Night"

"Blues in the Night" is a popular blues song which has become a pop standard and is generally considered to be part of the Great American Songbook. The music was written by Harold Arlen, the lyrics by Johnny Mercer, for a 1941 film begun with the working title Hot Nocturne, but finally released as Blues in the Night. In 1942 "Blues in the Night" was one of nine songs nominated for the Academy Award for Best Original Song. Observers expected that either "Blues in the Night" or "Chattanooga Choo Choo" would win, so that when "The Last Time I Saw Paris" actually won, neither its composer, Jerome Kern, nor lyricist, Oscar Hammerstein II, was present at the ceremony. The Woody Herman recording was released by Decca Records as catalogue number 4030. The record first reached the Billboard magazine charts on the 2nd January 1942 and lasted 11 weeks on the chart, peaking at #1.

Glenn Miller and His Orchestra with Ray Eberle and the Modernaires

"Moonlight Cocktail"

"Moonlight Cocktail" is a 1942 big band song recorded by Glenn Miller during World War II. The music was composed by Luckey Roberts with lyrics by Kim Gannon. The song was originally recorded by Glenn Miller and his Orchestra on December 8, 1941, the day after the attack on Pearl Harbor. The song had its first public performance in January 1942 on WABC radio in New York City. It was the best-selling record for ten weeks, from the 28th February 1942 to the 2nd May 1942 and was the number two record for that year after Bing Crosby's "White Christmas". During World War II, the BBC initiated a program called "Victory Through Harmony" that sought to use musical radio broadcasts to maintain wartime morale and increase weapons production. Some types of music were seen as a hindrance to such goals. Along with many other popular songs of the era, "Moonlight Cocktail" was banned by the BBC as "sentimental slush" in August 1942.

Jimmy Dorsey and His Orchestra with Bob Eberly and Helen O'Connell

"Tangerine"

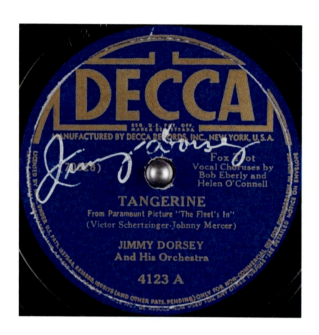

"**Tangerine**" is a popular song. The music was written by Victor Schertzinger, the lyrics by Johnny Mercer. It was introduced to a broad audience in the 1942 movie, The Fleet's In, produced by Paramount Pictures. The most popular recorded version of the song was made by the performers who introduced it in the film: The Jimmy Dorsey Orchestra with vocalists Helen O'Connell and Bob Eberly. The recording was released in January 1942 by Decca Records as catalogue number 4123. The record first reached the Billboard charts on the 10th April 1942, and lasted 15 weeks on the chart, including six weeks at #1. The lyrics in this version differ slightly from those in the movie. On the record, Eberly sings "And I've seen toasts to Tangerine / Raised in every bar across the Argentine," the lyric that became standard. In the movie at that point, the line is "And I've seen times when Tangerine / Had the bourgeoisie believing she were queen."

Harry James and his Orchestra

"Sleepy Logon"

"**Sleepy Logon**" The song, "Sleepy Lagoon", was published as a Lawrence-Coates collaboration in 1940. Lawrence showed the song to bandleader Harry James, whose recording of it was released by Columbia Records as catalogue number 36549. It first reached the Billboard Best Seller chart on the 17th April 1942 and lasted 18 weeks on the chart, peaking at number 1. Other hit versions were recorded by Dinah Shore, David Rose, Fred Waring, Glenn Miller and others. A recording with Tom Jenkins and his Palm Court Orchestra was made in London on the 15th March 1949. It was released by EMI on the His Master's Voice label as catalogue number B 9768. Peter Kreuder recorded the tune in 1949. The song made the Billboard Hot 100 in 1960, in a version by the Platters, found originally on the flipside of the 1960 top ten "Harbour Lights".

Kay Kyser and His Orchestra with Harry Babbitt, Julie Conway and the Group

"Jingle Jangle Jingle"

"Jingle Jangle Jingle" also known as 'I've Got Spurs That Jingle Jangle Jingle", is a song written by Joseph J. Lilley and Frank Loesser, and published in 1942. It was featured in that year's film The Forest Rangers, in which it was sung by Dick Thomas. The most commercially successful recording was by Kay Kyser, whose version reached no. 1 in the Billboard charts in July 1942.

The song was featured in the 1943 World War II-era theatrical Popeye the Sailor short Too Weak to Work, and was also sung by The Sportsmen Quartet: Bill Days (top tenor), Max Smith (second tenor), Mart Sperzel (baritone), and Gurney Bell (bass) in the 1942 Western movie Lost Canyon with Hopalong Cassidy (Bill Boyd).

Glenn Miller and His Orchestra with Tex Beneke, Marion Hutton and the Modernaires

"(I've Got a Gal In) Kalamazoo"

"(I've Got a Gal in) Kalamazoo" is a #1 popular song recorded by Glenn Miller and His Orchestra in 1942. It was written by Mack Gordon and Harry Warren and published in 1942. It was featured in the musical film Orchestra Wives and was recorded by Glenn Miller and His Orchestra, featuring Tex Beneke, Marion Hutton and The Modernaires, who released it as an A side 78 in 1942, 27934-A. The B side was "At Last".

The song popularized the city of Kalamazoo, Michigan. Although originally recorded by the Glenn Miller band with Tex Beneke on lead vocals, it was recreated by the fictional Gene Morrison Orchestra performing as the Glenn Miller Band and the Nicholas Brothers in the 1942 20th Century Fox movie Orchestra Wives. The song was nominated for Best Music, Original Song at the Academy Awards. The Glenn Miller record was the year's best-selling recording.

Bing Crosby with the Ken Darby Singers and John Scott Trotter and His Orchestra

"White Christmas"

"White Christmas" Bing Crosby recorded a version of the song for release as a single with the Kim Darby Singers and the John Scott Trotter Orchestra on the 29th May 1942 - a few months before the movie hit theatres. At the advice of Bing's record producer Jack Kapp, this original first verse was excised as it made no sense outside of the context of the film. Now starting with the familiar, "I'm dreaming of a white Christmas," the song became a huge hit, going to #1 on the Billboard chart in October, and staying in the top spot for 11 weeks, taking it through the first two weeks of 1943. The song enjoyed a sales resurgence every Christmas after it was first released in 1942. It went to #1 that year in America, and again reached the top spot in 1945 and 1947. The song appeared on various Billboard charts every year until 1963 when it finally dropped off the Hot 100.

Alton Glenn Miller was an American big-band trombonist, arranger, composer, and bandleader in the swing era. He was the best-selling recording artist from 1939 to 1942, leading one of the best-known big bands. Miller's recordings include "In the Mood", "Moonlight Serenade", "Pennsylvania 6-5000", "Chattanooga Choo Choo", "A String of Pearls", "At Last", "(I've Got a Gal In) Kalamazoo", "American Patrol", "Tuxedo Junction", "Elmer's Tune", and "Little Brown Jug". In just four years Glenn Miller scored 16 number-one records and 69 top ten hits—more than Elvis Presley (38 top 10s) and the Beatles (33 top 10s) did in their careers. While he was traveling to entertain U.S. troops in France during World War II, Miller's aircraft disappeared in bad weather over the English Channel.

WORLD EVENTS 1942

January

2 | Axis forces surrendered at Bardia, Libya. Some 2,200 German troops and 4,400 Italians were captured.

4 | Japanese aircraft carrier Chitose was bombed by B-17 Flying Fortresses off Davao City but damage sustained was negligible.

5 | Egypt broke off diplomatic relations with Bulgaria and Finland.

7 | The Battle of Moscow ended in strategic Soviet victory.

8 | Adolf Hitler had Generaloberst Erich Hoepner sacked for ordering his forces to pull back on the Eastern Front without approval. Hitler not only had Hoepner removed from command but deprived him of his pension and the right to wear his uniform as well.

10 | The gangster-themed thriller film All Through the Night starring Humphrey Bogart, Conrad Veidt and Kaaren Verne was released.

11 | The British cargo steamship Cyclops was torpedoed and sunk off the coast of Nova Scotia by German submarine U-123. It was the first attack of the Kriegsmarine's Operation Drumbeat aiming to destroy Allied shipping in the Western Atlantic.

13 | Representatives of nine governments in exile signed an agreement in London declaring that one of their principal war aims would be to ensure that those responsible for war crimes would be brought to justice.

16 | Prime Minister Winston Churchill became the first head of state to cross the Atlantic Ocean by plane, following the First Washington Conference with President Franklin Roosevelt.

19 | An Axis convoy docked at Tripoli providing Rommel with 55 new panzers, 20 armored cars, and a large quantity of fuel, food and ammunition. Rommel immediately began planning a new offensive.

21 | Sonderkommando Blaich: One Heinkel He 111 medium bombers raided the Free French-controlled Fort Lamy in French Equatorial Africa. The plane bombed the fort unchallenged but then ran low on fuel and had to make an emergency landing, leaving the crew stranded some 120 miles from their airstrip in southern Libya until a Junkers Ju 52 transport aircraft arrived a week later with fuel.

January

25 During the Battle of Borneo, the Japanese 56th Mixed Infantry Group captured the seaport city of Balikpapan.

27 Japanese submarine I-73 was torpedoed and sunk 240 miles west of Midway Atoll by the USS Gudgeon. This marked the first time in the war that a United States Navy submarine sank an enemy warship.

30 Adolf Hitler made a speech in the Berlin Sportpalast on the ninth anniversary of the Nazis coming to power. He declared, "We are fully aware that this war can end only either in the extermination of the Teutonic peoples or in the disappearance of Jewry from Europe." Hitler predicted that "the outcome of this war will be the annihilation of Jewry."

February

1 The Germans switched their naval codes from Hydra to the more complex Triton.

3 Erwin Rommel's forces captured Timimi in Libya. The British Eighth Army fell back and began establishing what would soon be known as the Gazala Line.

4 The U.K. Ministry of War Production was created and Lord Beaverbrook was appointed its first head.

6 German submarine U-82 was depth charged and sunk northeast of the Azores by British warships.

7 Rommel halted his counteroffensive near Gazala. In a little over two weeks he had retaken almost all the ground that the British Eighth Army had taken at the end of 1941.

10 A two-day meeting between Ion Antonescu and Adolf Hitler began at the Wolf's Lair. Antonescu pledged to commit large Romanian forces to the upcoming offensive on the Eastern Front but asked for modern equipment as a condition. Antonescu also warned that Romania still claimed all of Transylvania, but promised not to press this demand until the end of the war. Hitler was non-committal, but later instructed all German officials to be careful in their dealings with Hungary and Romania since both would be called upon to make more sacrifices for the Axis war effort.

11 Jacob Epstein's huge new sculpture depicting the Biblical story of Jacob wrestling with the angel went on show in London. His treatment of religious subject matter in a primitivist style was controversial for its time.

13 The German Navy completed the Channel Dash; they managed to avoid British air and naval attacks, but both battlecruisers were seriously damaged by British sea mines.

15 The Battle of Singapore ended in decisive Japanese victory. The Japanese occupation of Singapore began.

17 The Farrer Park address took place two days after the fall of Singapore when the British Malaya Command formally surrendered the Indian troops of the British Indian Army to Japanese Major Iwaichi Fujiwara. Authority was transferred in turn to the command of Mohan Singh, who addressed the gathered troops declaring the formation of the Indian National Army to fight the British Raj.

February

19 | Bombing of Darwin: 242 Japanese aircraft attacked the harbor and airfields around Darwin, Australia. The town was lightly defended and the Japanese inflicted heavy losses. Tanker British Motorist, cargo ships Don Isidro, Mauna Loa, Meigs, Neptuna and Zealandia, coal hulk Kelat, transport ship Portmar patrol boats Coongoola and Mavie and destroyers USS Peary and HNLMS Piet Hein were all sunk. Hajime Toyoshima crash-landed on Melville Island and became the first Japanese prisoner of war on Australian soil.

21 | Madame Chiang Kai-shek broadcast her husband's farewell message over Indian radio. "In these horrible times of savagery and brute force, the people of China and their brethren the people of India should, for the sake of civilization and human freedom, give their united support to the principles embodied in the Atlantic Charter and in the joint declaration of the 26 nations, and ally themselves with the anti-aggression front," the message read. "I hope the Indian people will wholeheartedly join the allies-namely, China, Great Britain, America and the Soviet Union-and participate shoulder to shoulder in the struggle for survival of a free world until complete victory has been achieved and the duties incumbent upon them in these troubled times have been fully discharged."

23 | Joseph Stalin marked the 24th anniversary of the founding of the Red Army with a statement broadcast to all Russians declaring that a "tremendous and hard fight" still lay ahead, but now that the Germans had spent the "element of surprise" the Soviets were taking the offensive and that "the Red banner will fly everywhere it has flown before."

27 | The British executed Operation Biting, an overnight attack on a German radar installation at Bruneval in northern France.

28 | The play Lady in Danger by Max Afford premiered at the Independent Theatre in Sydney, Australia.

March

1 | Construction of the Sobibór extermination camp began. As an extermination camp rather than a concentration camp, Sobibor existed for the sole purpose of killing Jews. The vast majority of prisoners were gassed within hours of arrival. Those not killed immediately were forced to assist in the operation of the camp, and few survived more than a few months. In total, some 170,000 to 250,000 people were murdered at Sobibor, making it the fourth-deadliest Nazi camp after Belzec, Treblinka, and Auschwitz.

March

3 | KNILM Douglas DC-3 shootdown: A Douglas DC-3 airliner was shot down over Australia by Japanese warplanes, resulting in the deaths of four passengers and the loss of diamonds worth an estimated A£ 150,000–300,000. The diamonds were presumably looted from the crash site but their fate remains a mystery.

6 | A controversial political cartoon by Philip Zec appeared in the Daily Mirror, depicting a merchant seaman clinging to the remains of a ship in rough seas with the caption, "The price of petrol has been increased by one penny – Official." Winston Churchill interpreted the cartoon as "defeatist" and considered acting to ban the Daily Mirror from publication.

9 | Slovak authorities required all Jews to wear the yellow badge.

11 | Brazilian President Getúlio Vargas by decree reiterated his powers to declare war or a state of national emergency, clearing the way for the seizure of subjects and property of Axis countries.

13 | The musical comedy film Song of the Islands starring Betty Grable and Victor Mature was released.

15 | Nazi occupying forces and local collaborationists committed the First Dünamünde Action in the Biķernieki forest near Riga, massacring about 1,900 people.

16 | Members of the far-right Swiss National Front were sentenced to long prison terms for propagandistic activities.

17 | The British government announced the introduction of fuel rationing.

21 | The last British cavalry charge in history occurred when about 60 Sikh sowars of the Burma Frontier Force attacked Japanese infantry at Taungoo. Most were killed.

22 | The BBC began transmitting news bulletins in Morse Code for the benefit of resistance fighters in occupied Europe.

24 | German submarine U-655 was rammed and sunk in the Barents Sea by the minesweeper HMS Sharpshooter.

March

25 Holocaust in Slovakia: The first mass transport of Jews to Auschwitz concentration camp departed from Poprad railway station in the Slovak Republic, consisting of 997 young women.

26 The Nazis began the deportation of Jews to Auschwitz concentration camp with the transport of 1,000 single women from Slovakia via Poprad transit camp. This was also the first deportation of Slovak Jews; of the 57,000 deported in 1942 only a few hundred survived the Holocaust.

28 Bombing of Lübeck: The port city of Lübeck was the first German city attacked in substantial numbers by the Royal Air Force. The night attack caused a firestorm that caused severe damage to the historic centre and led to the retaliatory Baedeker raids on historic British cities.

31 Allied convoy PQ 13 reached Murmansk despite fierce German attacks. PQ 13 was a British Arctic convoy that delivered war supplies from the Western Allies to the USSR during World War II. The convoy was subject to attack by German air, U-boat and surface forces and suffered the loss of five ships, plus one escort vessel. Fifteen ships arrived safely.

April

2 The comedy film My Favorite Blonde starring Bob Hope and Madeleine Carroll was released.

4 The Luftwaffe carried out Operation Eisstoß (Ice Assault) with the objective of smashing the Soviet fleet at Kronstadt, which was well-protected by anti-aircraft guns. 62 Stukas, 70 bombers and 50 Bf 109s were deployed and managed to inflict damage on thirteen Soviet warships, but not a single one was sunk.

7 A devastating air raid was conducted against the Maltese capital of Valletta. The Royal Opera House, one of the most beautiful buildings in the city, took a direct hit and was reduced to rubble.

8 The Canadian government created the Park Steamship Company to build Park ships, the Canadian equivalent of the American Liberty ships and British Fort ships.

10 Hotelier Conrad Hilton married Zsa Zsa Gabor at the Santa Fe Hotel in New Mexico.

12 The first units of the Hungarian 2nd Army left for the Eastern Front.

13 Byron Nelson won the Masters Tournament in a playoff against Ben Hogan. The Masters would not be played again until 1946.

14 On Budget Day in the United Kingdom, Chancellor of the Exchequer Kingsley Wood announced that Britain's war expenditures for the year ended March 31 totaled £4 billion, exceeding the estimate by £285 million. Wood projected expenditure for 1942–43 at £5.286 billion and raised taxes on non-essential goods and services such as alcohol, tobacco, cinema admissions and cosmetics.

21 Irish-American aviator Edward O'Hare became the first naval recipient of the Medal of Honor.

22 The Alfred Hitchcock-directed spy thriller film Saboteur starring Robert Cummings and Priscilla Lane premiered in Washington, D.C.

April

24	The comedy gangster film Larceny, Inc. starring Edward G. Robinson premiered in New York City.
25	16-year old Princess Elizabeth registered for war service.
26	The German Reichstag convened for what would be its final session. Chancellor Adolf Hitler gave a long speech asking for total legislative and judicial power that would give him the right to promote or punish anyone with no regard to legal procedures. The Reichstag agreed and Hitler was given absolute power of life and death.
27	All Jews in the Nazi-occupied Netherlands were ordered to wear the yellow badge.
29	Hitler met with Benito Mussolini at Salzburg for a conference on Axis war strategy. Mussolini agreed to send more Italian troops to the Eastern Front. The problem of what to do about Malta was also discussed, and plans for an invasion that would be codenamed Operation Herkules took shape.
30	Dzyatlava massacre: About 1,000 to 1,200 Jews were murdered by German authorities in the Kurpiesze forest near Dzyatlava.

May

1	Joseph Stalin published a message on International Workers' Day in which he stated that the Soviet Union was fighting a "patriotic war of liberation" and had no aim of "seizing foreign countries" or "conquering foreign peoples."
6	The British cargo ship Empire Buffalo was torpedoed and sunk west of the Cayman Islands by German submarine U-125.
8	The Philippines Campaign ended in decisive Japanese victory. The Japanese occupation of the Philippines began.
10	Winston Churchill gave a radio broadcast on the second anniversary of his being appointed British Prime Minister. Churchill warned the Germans that "we shall treat the unprovoked use of poison gas against our Russian ally exactly as if it were used against ourselves and if we are satisfied that this new outrage has been committed by Hitler we will use our great and growing air superiority in the West to carry gas warfare on the largest possible scale far and wide against military objectives in Germany. It is thus for Hitler to choose whether he wishes to add this additional horror to aerial warfare."
13	Action of 13 May 1942: Motor Torpedo Boats of the Royal Navy attempted to stop the German auxiliary cruiser Stier from reaching Gironde, France. Although Stier made it through the English Channel, two German torpedo boats were sunk with one British MTB lost in return.
18	An information appliances equipment brand, Epson was founded in Suwa, Nagano Prefecture, Japan. As predecessor name was Daiwa Kogyo.
21	The Mexican oil tanker Faja de Oro was torpedoed and sunk in the Gulf of Mexico by German submarine U-106. This incident along with the Potrero del Llano sinking on the 14th provided a casus belli for Mexico to declare war on the Axis.

May

22 | Townsville Mutiny: About 600 African-American servicemen mutinied in Townsville, Australia in reaction to being regularly subjected to racial abuse by some of their white officers. At least one person was killed and Australian troops were called in to roadblock the rioters.

23 | Hitler gave an address to senior Nazis in which he said that concentration camps were the main bulwark against an uprising.

24 | A 15-minute test blackout centered on Detroit was held starting at 10 p.m., with neighboring communities such as Pontiac and Windsor, Ontario also participating. It was the largest blackout in the Midwestern United States up to that time.

29 | Jews in Nazi-occupied Paris were ordered to wear the yellow badge starting June 7.

30 | In Operation Millennium, the British conducted a thousand-plane bombing raid on Cologne targeting the city's chemical and machine tool industries. Almost 1,500 tons of bombs were dropped in 90 minutes, killing 469 people and leaving 45,000 homeless.

June

2 | During the Siege of Sevastopol, the German 11th Army began a massive five-day artillery barrage on the fortress city using 620 guns including the enormous 800mm Schwerer Gustav "Dora" gun.

4 |

The Japanese aircraft carriers Akagi, Kaga and Sōryū were crippled in the Battle of Midway and scuttled.

June

5 The King's Birthday Honors 1942 were appointments by King George VI to various orders and honors to reward and highlight good works by members of the British Empire. They were published on 5 June 1942 for the United Kingdom and Canada. The recipients of honors are displayed here as they were styled before their new honor, and arranged by honor, with classes (Knight, Knight Grand Cross, etc.) and then divisions (Military, Civil, etc.) as appropriate.

7 British Commandos executed Operation Albumen, an overnight raid on German airfields on Axis-occupied Crete. The British managed to destroy 5 aircraft, damage 29 others and set fire to several vehicles and significant quantities of supplies.

8 The nine-day long Attack on Sydney Harbor by Japanese submarines ended indecisively.

10 The Czech village of Lidice was completely destroyed by German forces in reprisal for the assassination of Reinhard Heydrich. All men older than 15 years were executed. Most of children were executed later.

12 Anne Frank received a diary for her thirteenth birthday.

16 The war film Eagle Squadron starring Robert Stack, Diana Barrymore, John Loder and Nigel Bruce was released.

17 Japanese Prime Minister Hideki Tojo was slightly wounded when a Korean nationalist shot him in the left arm outside the old war ministry building in Tokyo. Japanese police returned fire and killed the man identified as 31-year old Park Soowon. The incident was not revealed to the public for two months.

18 Charles de Gaulle gave a speech at the Royal Albert Hall in London praising the unity of the Resistance movements.

20 The comic book villain Two-Face made his first appearance in Detective Comics issue #66

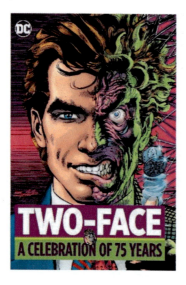 

22 Erwin Rommel was promoted to the rank of field marshal as a reward for his victory in the Battle of Gazala.

June

23 Albert Speer told Hitler that nuclear science would reap benefits in the distant future, but no superbomb could be produced in time to affect the war. The German military decided to abandon nuclear research as a result. That same day, Werner Heisenberg almost died when his experimental reactor at Leipzig suffered a leak that started a fire. Heisenberg and his assistant Robert Döpel extinguished the fire but noticed the sphere was beginning to swell, and both men ran outside before the reactor exploded and the lab was destroyed. Rumor spread that the scientists had been killed in a uranium bomb explosion, and when word of it reached the scientists working on the Manhattan Project, they assumed that the Germans had achieved a sustained nuclear chain reaction and were considerably further ahead in their research than they actually were.

26 The German 11th Army opened its assault on the inner defenses of Sevastopol.

30 All remaining Jewish schools were closed in Germany.

July

1 44 Japanese were killed by Australian commandos in the Raid on Heath's Farm in New Guinea.

2 Following two weeks of reverses on the North African front, a motion of censure was brought against Winston Churchill in the House of Commons proposing that "this House, while paying tribute to the heroism and endurance of the Armed Forces of the Crown in circumstances of exceptional difficulty, has no confidence in the central direction of the war." Churchill gave a lengthy speech before the vote, conceding that the campaign in North Africa had not been going well but insisting that things would improve once vast amounts of American military supplies arrived. The motion was defeated, 475 to 25.

3 Russian authorities admitted the loss of Sevastopol but claimed that its capture had cost the Germans 300,000 casualties.

6 The American League defeated the National League 3-1 in the 10th Major League Baseball All-Star Game at the Polo Grounds in New York City. It was the first night game in All-Star history.

July

7 | Heinrich Himmler authorized sterilization experiments to take place at Auschwitz concentration camp.

8 | One week after gaining U.S. citizenship, the British-born movie star Cary Grant married the socialite heiress Barbara Hutton at Lake Arrowhead, California.

11 | RAF Lancaster bombers flew the longest raid of the European theatre up to this time, traveling 1,750 miles to bomb German shipyards at Danzig.

14 | Two women were shot dead in Marseille when an enormous crowd gathered illegally for Bastille Day, waving French flags and singing "La Marseillaise". Charles de Gaulle led Bastille Day celebrations of his own in London.

16 | In the First Battle of El Alamein, Australian forces were repelled on an attempt to take Point 24 from the Germans and suffered nearly fifty percent casualties.

18 | The Messerschmitt Me 262 had its first test flight with jet engines.

26 | During the First Battle of El Alamein, British troops launched Operation Manhood in a final attempt to break the Axis forces.

27 | The First Battle of El Alamein ended in stalemate but a strategic Allied victory.

28 | Arthur Harris made a radio broadcast informing German listeners that the bombers would soon be coming "every night and every day, rain, blow or snow - we and the Americans. I have just spent eight months in America, so I know exactly what is coming. We are going to scourge the Third Reich from end to end, if you make it necessary for us to do so ... it is up to you to end the war and the bombing. You can overthrow the Nazis and make peace."

31 | 630 British bombers raided Düsseldorf, destroying 453 buildings and killing 276 civilians. 29 bombers were lost.

August

2   After spending most of the day studying maps of Stalingrad and the surrounding area, Andrey Yeryomenko had a second conference with Stalin. Yeryomenko protested that two Russian fronts in the same area meant that trying to co-ordinate Stalingrad's defense with another commander would be "utterly confusing, if not tragically impossible," and asked to command the Stalingrad Front in the north rather than the Southeastern Front. Stalin firmly said that everything would be left as it was already outlined.

5   Anthony Eden announced in the House of Commons that the Munich Agreement of 1938 would play no part in the postwar settlement of Czechoslovakia's borders, because the British government no longer considered itself bound to that agreement since the Germans destroyed it.

7   Winston Churchill visited the British troops at El Alamein.

9   The Walt Disney animated film Bambi had its world premiere in London.

13   Bernard Montgomery took over command of the British Eighth Army following the death of William Gott.

Bernard Montgomery   **William Gott**

14   British Commandos carried out Operation Barricade, an overnight raid on an anti-aircraft gun and radar site northwest of Pointe de Saire, France.

17   1,700 Jews are massacred in the Polish village of Łomazy by Reserve Police Battalion 101.

19   The Dieppe Raid took place on the northern coast of France. The operation was virtually a complete failure and almost 60% of the 6,086 men who made it ashore were killed, wounded or captured. The British destroyer Berkeley was crippled by Focke-Wulf Fw 190s and scuttled.

23   The German 16th Panzer Division came within striking distance of the Stalingrad Tractor Factory, the Soviet Union's largest producer of T-34 tanks.

25   A citywide evacuation effort began in Stalingrad. First priority went to specialists and workers whose factories had been destroyed.

29   The German Tiger I tank made its battlefield debut southeast of Leningrad.

September

1 | The German 4th Panzer Army attacked the Soviet 64th Army in the southern suburbs of Stalingrad.

5 | The Soviet 24th and 66th Armies counterattacked the XIV Panzer Corps at Stalingrad, but the offensive was called off after losing 30 of 120 tanks, mostly to the Luftwaffe.

10 | The RAF dropped 100,000 bombs on Düsseldorf in less than an hour.

13 | The Allies launched Operation Agreement, a series of ground and amphibious operations carried out by British, Rhodesian and New Zealand forces against Axis-held Tobruk.

17 | The British war film In Which We Serve, directed by Noël Coward and David Lean, was released in the United Kingdom.

20 | Allied commanders set November 8 as D-Day for Operation Torch. Operation Torch was an Allied invasion of French North Africa during the Second World War. While the French colonies formally aligned with Germany via Vichy France, the loyalties of the population were mixed. Reports indicated that they might support the Allies.

22 | The Germans occupied the center of Stalingrad.

23 | Erwin Rommel left North Africa on sick leave, handing over command of the Afrika Korps to Georg Stumme.

24 | German forces in Stalingrad broke through to the Volga River and cut the 62nd Army in two.

25 | The aviation-themed action film Desperate Journey starring Errol Flynn and Ronald Reagan was released.

26 | The Manhattan Project was granted approval by the War Production Board to use the highest level of emergency procurement priority.

27 | German submarine U-165 was depth charged and sunk in the Bay of Biscay by a Vickers Wellington aircraft of No. 311 Squadron RAF.

28 | Joseph Stalin signed an instruction ordering the resumption of the Soviet nuclear research program which had been dormant for a year.

30 | Hitler gave a speech in the Berlin Sportpalast informing his audience that "it will not be the Aryan peoples, but rather Jewry, that will be exterminated."

October

1 | The British Army - formed the new unit, Royal Electrical and Mechanical Engineers. (REME)

2 | Former French Prime Minister Édouard Herriot was arrested for allegedly plotting against the Vichy government.

October

6	A law was passed in Nazi-occupied Belgium equivalent to the one passed in Vichy France on September 4, obligating able-bodied citizens to do work for the government if ordered to.
8	A Nazi radio announcement stated that officers and men captured in the Dieppe raid had been manacled in retaliation for the alleged tying of prisoners during the Sark raid. The British War Office replied that German prisoners of war captured at Dieppe had not had their hands tied and if the Germans did not immediately unshackle their prisoners, then German POWs in Canada would be put in chains starting October 10.
10	Battle of Bowmanville: A revolt in the Bowmanville POW camp in Ontario, Canada broke out. 400 prisoners barricaded themselves in a hall in protest of the intended shackling of 126 prisoners as reprisal for the chaining of Canadian soldiers captured at Dieppe.
13	The V2 rocket (number V4) becomes the first man-made object to be launched into space.
16	A cyclone from the Bay of Bengal reportedly killed 40,000 people, with particularly heavy damage around Contai.
18	Adolf Hitler issued the Commando Order stating that all Allied commandos encountered by German forces should be killed immediately without trial, even if they were in proper uniforms or attempted to surrender.
23	The Second Battle of El Alamein was a battle of the Second World War that took place near the Egyptian railway halt of El Alamein. The First Battle of El Alamein and the Battle of Alam el Halfa had prevented the Axis from advancing further into Egypt.

24	Operations of the German 6th Army in Stalingrad slowed down considerably due to exhaustion after two weeks of intense fighting as well as the weather growing appreciably colder.
28	12 Hawker Hurricanes under the command of Greek aviator Ioannis Kellas marked Ohi Day by raiding Italian positions at El Alamein.
29	Leading British clergymen and political figures held a public meeting to express their outrage at the persecution of Jews by Nazi Germany. Churchill sent a message to the meeting stating that "Free men and women denounce these vile crimes, and when this world struggle ends with the enthronement of human rights, racial persecution will be ended."

November

2 The BBC began French-language broadcasts to Canada.

3 Erwin Rommel received an order from Adolf Hitler to "stand and die", but disregarded it as plans for a withdrawal were already in place.

5 Fighting in and around Stalingrad forced the city's power plant to shut down.

7 Joseph Stalin issued an Order of the Day on the 25th anniversary of the October Revolution promising that the enemy "will yet feel the weight of the Red Army's smashing blows."

8 Hitler made his annual speech in Munich on the 19th anniversary of the Beer Hall Putsch. Hitler claimed that Stalingrad was in German hands with only "a few small pockets" of resistance left.

10 Winston Churchill took to the podium at the Lord Mayor's Luncheon in London with news of the Allied victory at El Alamein. "Now this is not the end," Churchill said. "It is not even the beginning of the end. But it is, perhaps, the end of the beginning."

11 The Second Battle of El Alamein ended in decisive Allied victory.

13 Montgomery captured Tobruk, squeezing Rommel between two large advancing Allied forces.

15 Church bells were rung throughout England in celebration of the Allied victory at El Alamein. It was the first time that church bells had sounded since 1940 when they were silenced during the threat of German invasion.

19 Operation Freshman: A British airborne force landed using gliders in Norway with the intent of sabotaging a chemical plant in Telemark that the Germans could use for their atomic weapons programme. Neither of the two aircraft-glider forces were able to land near their objective and the operation ended in failure with 41 killed.

21 The character of Tweety Bird first appeared in the Warner Bros. cartoon A Tale of Two Kitties.

23 Operation Uranus ended in decisive Soviet victory with the German 6th Army completely encircled at Stalingrad.

25 The Germans began airlifting supplies to the 6th Army trapped in Stalingrad. Only 47 Ju 52 transport planes were on hand for the first day, a small fraction of what was needed. Hermann Göring ordered as many Ju 52s as possible to be requisitioned from around occupied Europe to join in the operation.

27 The French fleet in Toulon was scuttled to keep it out of the hands of German forces. 3 battleships, 7 cruisers, 15 destroyers, 12 submarines and 13 torpedo boats were among the ships scuttled.

29 Churchill made a radio broadcast reviewing the state of the war and suggesting that the Italian people faced a choice between enduring "prolonged scientific and shattering air attack" from North Africa or overthrowing Mussolini.

December

2 | Benito Mussolini addressed the Chamber of Fasces and Corporations for the first time in eighteen months, reporting on the present state of the war and insisting that "The last word has not yet been spoken." Mussolini advised the population to evacuate Italian cities, causing a panic as there was no planning or organization to do it.

4 | American planes bombed Italy for the first time when 20 B-24s raided Naples.

6 | 93 aircraft of the Royal Air Force conducted a daylight bombing raid on Eindhoven targeting the Philips Radio Works. The building was heavily damaged but the RAF lost 13 planes in the attack.

7 | Operation Frankton: A small unit of Royal Marines began raiding shipping in the French port of Bordeaux.

10 | German tank infantry columns attacked Majaz al Bab in Tunisia but were repulsed.

12 | 99 civilians and military personnel perished in the Knights of Columbus Hostel fire in St. John's, Newfoundland. The fire was likely an incidence of enemy sabotage carried out by Nazi agents.

13 | Rommel withdrew for Tunisia despite Hitler's insistence that he make a stand at El Agheila.

17 | The Volga River finally froze over, allowing Soviet forces in Stalingrad to be resupplied.

18 | Benito Mussolini sent Galeazzo Ciano to meet with Hitler at the Wolf's Lair. Ciano carried Mussolini's message urging Hitler to seek a separate peace with the Soviets, but Hitler strongly rejected the idea.

23 | Operation Winter Storm ended with the German 6th Army still trapped in the Stalingrad pocket.

24 | The Soviet 62nd Army retook the Red October factory in Stalingrad.

26 | Rommel halted at Buerat, where he was ordered by Mussolini to make a stand.

27 | The fifth National Football League All-Star Game was held at Shibe Park in Philadelphia. An all-star team defeated the Washington Redskins 17–14.

28 | Hitler issued Directive No. 47, concerning command and defense measures in the southeast. The directive referred to the possibility of attacks in the region of Crete and the Balkans.

29 | The Soviets retook Kotelnikovo south of Stalingrad.

30 | Frank Sinatra performed his first solo concert at the Paramount Theatre in New York City. Sinatra later recalled being "scared stiff" when the audience of 5,000 bobby soxers shrieked and screamed continuously for America's new teen idol.

31 | Hitler issued an Order of the Day to the German armed forces declaring, "The year 1943 will perhaps be hard but certainly not harder than the one just behind us."

PEOPLE IN POWER

John Curtin
1941-1945
Australia
Prime Minister

Philippe Pétain
1940-1944
France
Président

Getúlio Vargas
1930-1945
Brazil
President

William Mackenzie King
1935-1948
Canada
Prime Minister

Lin Sen
1931-1943
China
Government of China

Adolf Hitler
1934-1945
Germany
Führer of Germany

Marquess of Linlithgow
1936-1943
India
Viceroy of India

Benito Mussolini
1922-1943
Italy
President

Hiroito
1926-1989
Japan
Emperor

Manuel Ávila Camacho
1940-1946
Mexico
President

Joseph Stalin
1922-1952
Russia
Premier

Jan Smuts
1939-1948
South Africa
Prime Minister

Franklin D. Roosevelt
1933-1945
United States
President

Hubert Pierlot
1939-1945
Belgium
Prime Minister

Peter Fraser
1939-1949
New Zealand
Prime Minister

Sir Winston Churchill
1940-1945
United Kingdom
Prime Minister

Per Albin Hansson
1936-1946
Sweden
Prime Minister

Christian X
1912-1947
Denmark
King

Francisco Franco
1936-1975
Spain
President

Miklós Horthy
1920-1944
Hungary
Kingdom of Hungary

The Year You Were Born 1942
Book by Sapphire Publishing

Made in the USA
Las Vegas, NV
14 July 2024

92303808R00052